Editor-in-Chief and Founder:
  Lyndon H. LaRouche, Jr.
Editorial Board: *Lyndon H. LaRouche, Jr. , Helga
  Zepp-LaRouche, Robert Ingraham, Tony
  Papert, Gerald Rose, Dennis Small, Jeffrey
  Steinberg, William Wertz*
Co-Editors: *Robert Ingraham, Tony Papert*
Technology: *Marsha Freeman*
Books: *Katherine Notley*
Ebooks: *Richard Burden*
Graphics: *Alan Yue*
Photos: *Stuart Lewis*
Circulation Manager: *Stanley Ezrol*

INTELLIGENCE DIRECTORS
Counterintelligence: *Jeffrey Steinberg, Michele
  Steinberg*
Economics: *John Hoefle, Marcia Merry Baker,
  Paul Gallagher*
History: *Anton Chaitkin*
Ibero-America: *Dennis Small*
Russia and Eastern Europe: *Rachel Douglas*
United States: *Debra Freeman*

INTERNATIONAL BUREAUS
Bogotá: *Miriam Redondo*
Berlin: *Rainer Apel*
Copenhagen: *Tom Gillesberg*
Houston: *Harley Schlanger*
Lima: *Sara Madueño*
Melbourne: *Robert Barwick*
Mexico City: *Gerardo Castilleja Chávez*
New Delhi: *Ramtanu Maitra*
Paris: *Christine Bierre*
Stockholm: *Ulf Sandmark*
United Nations, N.Y.C.: *Leni Rubinstein*
Washington, D.C.: *William Jones*
Wiesbaden: *Göran Haglund*

ON THE WEB
e-mail: eirns@larouchepub.com
www.larouchepub.com
www.executiveintelligencereview.com
www.larouchepub.com/eiw
Webmaster: *John Sigerson*
Assistant Webmaster: *George Hollis*
Editor, Arabic-language edition: *Hussein Askary*

EIR (ISSN 0273-6314) *is published weekly
(50 issues), by EIR News Service, Inc.,
P.O. Box 17390, Washington, D.C. 20041-0390.
(703) 297-8434*

European Headquarters: E.I.R. GmbH, Postfach
Bahnstrasse 9a, D-65205, Wiesbaden, Germany
Tel: 49-611-73650
Homepage: http://www.eir.de
e-mail: info@eir.de
Director: Georg Neudecker

Montreal, Canada: 514-461-1557
eir@eircanada.ca

Denmark: EIR - Danmark, Sankt Knuds Vej 11,
basement left, DK-1903 Frederiksberg, Denmark.
Tel.: +45 35 43 60 40, Fax: +45 35 43 87 57. e-mail:
eirdk@hotmail.com.

Mexico City: EIR, Sor Juana Inés de la Cruz 242-2
Col. Agricultura C.P. 11360
Delegación M. Hidalgo, México D.F.
Tel. (5525) 5318-2301
eirmexico@gmail.com

Copyright: ©2017 EIR News Service. All rights
reserved. Reproduction in whole or in part without
permission strictly prohibited.

Canada Post Publication Sales Agreement
#40683579

Postmaster: Send all address changes to *EIR*, P.O.
Box 17390, Washington, D.C. 20041-0390.

Signed articles in *EIR* represent the views of the authors,
and not necessarily those of the Editorial Board.

To Prevent a War, Break The 'Russiagate' Coup

Mueller's Russiagate Scam Is Imploding, So Neocons Are Hell Bent on War

Jan. 23—There should be no misunderstanding that the two contradictory courses of developments within the United States today are somehow merely a coincidence.

On the one hand, the two-year long campaign to stop Donald Trump, the so-called "Russiagate," orchestrated by British intelligence agent Christopher Steele and his assets within the Obama intelligence community, is now verging on collapse. The outright criminal actions by this conspiratorial cabal now stand exposed—and many of them should end up in prison. Peter Strzok, who led much of the Russia investigation at the FBI, and as a member of Robert Mueller's Russiagate task force, has been caught bragging in a text message to his lover (and fellow FBI agent) about a "secret society" to bring down Trump just after his election. Strzok was also exposed as expressing his belief that there was no substance to the charges of Russia collusion, even as he was joining the Mueller witchhunt.

On the other hand, the neoconservative hawks on both sides of the aisle, and in London, and even within Trump's immediate circle, have unleashed a shrill cry to prepare for war against the fake "threats" from Russia and China. The Chinese have taken note of the danger, while the Russians have more than taken note. There are multiple warnings from every part of the Russian establishment that the West appears to have gone mad—that despite Trump's clear and repeated calls for peaceful and friendly relations with Russia, the drive for war is rapidly approaching the point of no return.

At the Davos World Economic Summit, which opened today, Andrei Kostin, chief executive of VTB, one of Russia's leading banks, told the *Financial Times* that his biggest concern was the dangerous situation being created by the Nato build-up of arms in Europe, which risked an "accident" between Nato and Russian forces. Kostin said: "We are at the beginning of a new arms race." Kostin is said to be close to Putin. "Nato is asking for more weapons and spreading more weapons in Europe, and Russia will retaliate in absolutely the same way." Former U.S. Defense Secretary William Perry has made the same point—that the "launch on command" posture and the reckless U.S. military buildup in both Europe and the Pacific has brought the world closer to war than it ever was during the Cold War.

Kostin issued another warning, in light of threats from the U.S. Congress of yet more sanctions on Russia: "Any economic sanctions against institutions, personally I say, would be like declaring a war. I see no reason why the Russian Ambassador should stay in Washington any longer after that, or the American Ambassador staying, swimming in cold water in Moscow. I think that is a 'worse than the cold war' situation, and that is very dangerous. And I think that Congress is playing with fire, because the relationship is going from bad to worse and we are not responsible for that."

There is only one way to end the madness. The geopolitical blinders must be ripped from the eyes of the American and European populations, and especially their leaders. The new paradigm for humanity, long proposed by Lyndon and Helga LaRouche, is no longer simply a vision of the future—it is right before us, in the New Silk Road, already transforming the majority of nations in the world: in Asia, in Africa, in Ibero-America, and even in parts of Europe and the United States. To ascribe evil intent to this transformation, which rests on close cooperation between China and Russia in both economic and strategic matters, is pure madness. There is nothing holding back the Western nations from full participation in this new organization of relations in the world—not being replaced as the dominant power by the rising powers (as the geopolitical true believers in a unipolar world would have it), but as full partners in a partnership of sovereign nations committed to one common vision, for a better destiny for mankind.

The exposure by the LaRouche Political Action Committee of the British-orchestrated "Russiagate" as an attempted coup against the government of the United States has now burst into the public eye, but the financial Lords of the City of London and Wall Street would prefer war to accepting the end of their Imperial domain. This fight can be won, but the desperation of the dying species known as the oligarchy leaves little time to achieve this great transformation. The time for action by all good souls is now.

EIR Contents www.larouchepub.com Volume 45, Number 4, January 26, 2018

Robert Mueller

FBI

BREAKTHROUGH AGAINST GEOPOLITICS

The Stakes Are Very High Over the Coming Days

Matthew Ogden's weekly LaRouche PAC Monday Update webcast can be seen at https://larouchepac. com. *This Jan. 22 edition is on YouTube at* youtu.be/ NO3CBVoinsQ. *The transcript has been edited.*

Matthew Ogden: Good afternoon. It's January 22, 2018. My name is Matthew Ogden, and you're joining us for our Monday afternoon weekly strategic update here from larouchepac.com.

As you can see on our screen, we are now eight days from the official President Trump State of the Union address. We've been continuing this countdown, and this is scheduled, at least currently, for a week from tomorrow, Jan. 30, where President Trump will address a Joint Session of Congress in his first official State of the Union address. As you can see here by our graphic, our two agenda items continue to be LaRouche's Four Economic Laws and for the United States to join the New Silk Road. This is the subject of "The Campaign to Win the Future."

This is LaRouche PAC's policy platform for the year 2018, and we are engaged in a national mobilization to gain endorsements for this platform. Those endorsements can come from everybody—from private citizens, labor organizations, farm organizations, elected officials, and most importantly, from candidates for Federal, state, and local office. This is our campaign to shape the terms of the debate for the 2018 elections, and the more that we do over the coming eight days, between now and January 30th, the more impact we will have on the policy of the U.S. Presidency.

During this period, I guarantee you the news is going to be filled with all of the details and the melodrama about the government shutdown, and other things which are really side-issues. You can get lost in all of the details, and you can come to think of this as just partisanship and a Republican versus Democrat kind of partisan battle. But the real war which is being waged in Washington, is not what it seems. It's not this war between the Republicans and the Democrats over the so-called government shutdown. The real war in Washington, and which continues to escalate, is the war over the U.S. Presidency. Will it continue to exist at all, or will it be swept away in a coup involving fake charges of Russian collusion? Will President Trump be freed from the pressure of an illegal insurgency, so that he can move into full cooperation with Russia and China, and will he be supported to take the urgent steps outlined in "The Campaign to Win the Future"?

As Helga Zepp-LaRouche warned over this weekend, we are in very dangerous waters. We have not reached safe harbor yet as to what U.S. policy will be, especially U.S. policy on the world stage. As you know, Helga Zepp-LaRouche, at the beginning of this year, on January 1st—New Year's Day—declared that 2018 must be the year that we end geopolitics and inaugurate a new era of great power collaboration, great power partnerships, which must be built on a new philosophy of "win-win" cooperation. The leading great powers on this planet right now obviously are the United States, Russia, and China. If those three countries can create a win-win collaboration, the entire 20th Century paradigm of geopolitics, which has brought us to the threshold of thermonuclear war—that can be ended. As we know, President Trump has shown his intention to achieve that, especially in terms of a constructive relationship with Russia and with China.

However, directly contrary to that intention, over the weekend, the official National Defense Strategy was released, and it is full of inflammatory attacks on both Russia and on China. This National Defense Strategy goes so far as to call for a new era of great power competition, as opposed to what Helga Zepp-LaRouche called for, an era of great power cooperation. Literally, a revival of Cold War geopolitics. U.S. Defense Secretary James Mattis stated in a speech on Friday, an-

DoD/Navy Mass Communication Specialist 1st Class Kathryn E. Hold

U.S. Secretary of Defense James N. Mattis announces the National Defense Strategy at Johns Hopkins University School of Advanced International Studies in Washington, D.C., Jan. 19, 2018.

nouncing the release of this National Defense Strategy, the following: "We will continue to prosecute the campaign against terrorists that we have engaged in today. But great power competition, not terrorism, is now the primary focus of U.S. national security. We face growing threats from revisionist powers as different as China and Russia. Nations that seek to create a world consistent with their authoritarian models, pursuing veto authority over other nations' economic, diplomatic, and security decisions."

Now, this is clearly inflammatory and is stuck in the paradigm of Cold War geopolitics. What Helga Zepp-LaRouche has warned is that this is not just Cold War, but this kind of rhetoric or this kind of policy could literally lead to a hot war. What she emphasized is that we have to understand that this is very dangerous language.

Let me read some quotes from the National Security Directive, published as James Mattis announced its release during the speech that I just quoted from. Here's what is in this National Defense Strategy:

The central challenge to U.S. prosperity and se-

curity is the re-emergence of long-term, strategic competition by what the National Security Strategy classifies as revisionist powers. It is increasingly clear that China and Russia want to shape a world consistent with their authoritarian model—gaining veto authority over other nations' economic, diplomatic, and security decisions.

Concurrently, Russia seeks veto authority over nations on its periphery in terms of their governmental, economic, and diplomatic decisions, to shatter the North Atlantic Treaty Organization and change European and Middle East security and economic structures to its favor.

Another change to the strategic environment is a resilient, but weakening, post-World War II international order. China and Russia are now undermining the international order from within the system. For decades the United States has enjoyed uncontested or dominant superiority in every operating domain.

[We must] remain the pre-eminent military power in the world, [and] ensure the balances of power remain in our favor

Long-term strategic competitions with China and Russia are the principal priorities for the Department [of Defense].

Defense objectives include:

Maintaining favorable regional balances of power in the Indo-Pacific, Europe, the Middle East, and the Western Hemisphere.

So, this directly calls for great power competition, and asserts that the objective of U.S. policy will be to maintain military and strategic and economic hegemony over the entire world. Literally the opposite of what Zepp-LaRouche has called for, namely, the end of geopolitics, and the opposite of what President Xi Jinping has offered in terms of win-win great power collaborations in which you have not a winner take all, but mutual benefit for all powers involved, economic, strategic, and military.

Zepp-LaRouche issued a tweet over the weekend directly in response to this National Defense Strategy. This is what she said: "President Trump should revoke the new national security strategy document immediately, fire Mattis, and appoint Tulsi Gabbard as Defense Secretary. Signed, Helga Zepp-LaRouche." So, that tweet came directly from her, and she calls for President Trump to revoke the National Security document, fire Mattis, and instead, install Tulsi Gabbard in his place as Defense Secretary.

Nuclear War or Common Destiny?

As many of our viewers and supporters probably know, Tulsi Gabbard has been very vocal about the utter failure of the Cold War regime change policy of the United States. Gabbard, of course, is the Democratic Congresswoman from the state of Hawaii. Her warnings have only become more urgent in the wake of the false alarm—so-called—of an incoming ballistic missile in Hawaii.

This "false alarm," as you can see here on the screen, told people that they were about to be incinerated in a nuclear attack on Hawaii, and that they should immediately find shelter and take cover. It said, "Ballistic missile threat inbound to Hawaii. Seek immediate shelter. This is not a drill." And this is what was received by all Hawaii cell phones and everybody in that state, and was not revoked for 38 minutes. You can imagine the kind of environment of terror that reigned in the state of Hawaii for those 38 minutes.

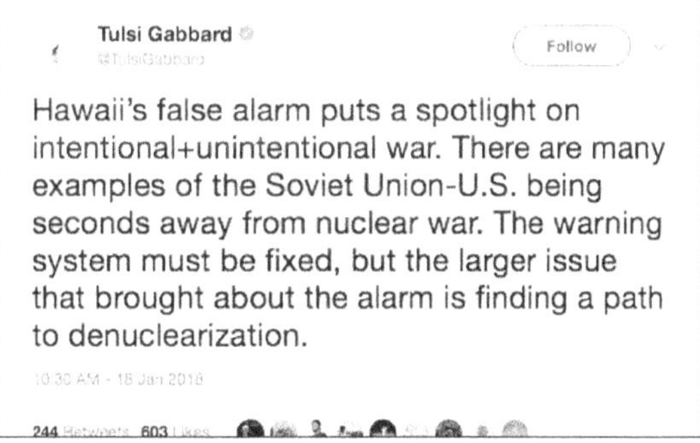

Now Gabbard found out about this and immediately tweeted out, once she discovered that it was indeed false, that "There is no incoming missile threat. This is a false alarm. This has been confirmed that there is no danger." But again, this was a false warning that was received by every single person who was in Hawaii at that moment.

Gabbard has been emphasizing that this should not be written off as some sort of "false alarm," but must be a wake-up call for the United States to immediately abandon the Cold War regime-change policies that led to this situation, and to "end the dark shadow of potential nuclear war." Here are a few examples of what she has been saying on Twitter in the past few days:

"Over a million of Hawaii's people were faced with the immediate reality of having 15 minutes to find a place to take shelter, wondering 'Where do I go? What shelter is going to protect me and family from a nuclear bomb?' But there's nowhere to go. Nowhere to hide." She said, "The people of Hawaii experienced that in 15 minutes, they and their families are going to be dead; gone. That's what they just went through." She said, "We have seen this nuclear threat during the Cold War, when the Soviet Union and the United States were seconds away from such an attack. Peace with North Korea requires immediate and direct talks without preconditions. Regime-change war policy is the reason why North Korea sees nuclear weapons as their only deterrent from a U.S.-led attack. Kim Jong-un sees what the United States has done to Qaddafi in Libya, Saddam Hussein in Iraq, and the effort underway to decertify the nuclear deal with Iran."

She said, "It was a mistake for the United States to take out Qaddafi and Hussein. Libya and Iraq are still reeling from the effects of our attacks. We need to learn from our mistakes; end our policy of regime change; and implement a policy of de-escalation and peace."

So, that's very explicit and very direct. As Gabbard says, we must end regime change; we need a new strategy of de-escalation and peace. You can see why Helga Zepp-LaRouche would call for her to be appointed Defense Secretary to replace James Mattis in the wake of the release of this so-called National Defense Strategy. It's completely contrary to what he is saying; this bellicose, geopolitical, neo-con line that's being taken by

DoD/Glenn Fawcett

Former Secretary of Defense Dr. William Perry (1994-1997), on March 6, 2015.

Mattis and others in his faction within the Trump administration.

Also in direct contradiction to Secretary Mattis, Zepp-LaRouche emphasized the statements of former Defense Secretary William Perry, and his response to the so-called false alarm in Hawaii. Here's a tweet that he posted *before* the "false alarm" in Hawaii. This was on January 3. He said, "We are at greater risk of nuclear catastrophe now than we were during the Cold War. We have ignored the existential threat of nuclear weapons for too long. The risk has always been there, and it will continue unless we take action." So that was prior to this incident in Hawaii. Following the incident, Perry published an article titled, "The Terrifying Lessons of Hawaii's Botched Missile Alert." Here's what he said in the article:

> "This is not a drill," announced the emergency alert, and for 37 minutes, hundreds of thousands of Hawaiians and tourists were left to contemplate the possibility that an incoming missile might soon end their lives.
>
> The consequences in Hawaii were that people were terrified. They were terrified not only because they thought that they and their families were going to die, but because they had no idea of "what to do."
>
> That they didn't know what to do is fundamental to a nuclear attack, especially if the missile is carrying a hydrogen bomb. One hydrogen bomb could kill essentially everyone in a city like Honolulu or Hilo, even if the residents took cover. So the "what to do" has to happen *before* the missile is fired. The way to save yourself and your family from being killed in a nuclear war is to keep such a war from happening. Once the missiles are launched, it is too late. And that is one important lesson we could learn from the Hawaii false alert.
>
> But there is also a second lesson. If the attack alert came from our military warning system, the president would be faced immediately with an existential decision. He would have 5 to 10 minutes to decide whether to launch our ICBMs before they were destroyed in their silos.
>
> If he decides to launch them, and it is a false alert, there will be no way to call them back or abort them in flight. He will have mistakenly started World War III, a war likely to destroy our civilization.
>
> [T]he consequence of a mistaken launch order is no less than the end of our civilization as we know it. That is the problem we face, and no "duck-and-cover" drills can solve it, or even mitigate it. Instead, we need to get serious about re-engaging the Russians on ways of reducing nuclear dangers to both of us; we need to give up our "launch on warning" policy. All of these actions will be hard to execute, but the possible consequences of failure are so great that we have a responsibility to give them our highest priority.

What William Perry is warning about, is exactly what Lyndon LaRouche was involved in trying to prevent when he worked with President Ronald Reagan in the early 1980s to draft what became known as the Strategic Defense Initiative. This was not just missile defense in some sort of simplistic unilateral way; it was a joint program of space-based missile defense based on cutting-edge plasma and laser beam technology. Lyndon LaRouche was actively involved in working with leading layers inside the diplomatic community in Russia, to say, "Let us adopt this as a joint program. The United States and Russia must jointly adopt this Strategic Defense Initiative in order to end the threat of thermonuclear war once and for all." That was President Reagan's intention when he announced the Strategic Defense Initiative on March 23, 1983. But it was not adopted by both sides, and if it had been, we wouldn't be living under this nuclear sword of Damocles as we are today.

Tulsi Gabbard and William Perry are warning today that the threat of thermonuclear war is all too real, and that we must urgently change our policies. What Gabbard said is that we have to declare an end to the policy of regime change. Perry said we "need to get serious about re-engaging the Russians on ways of reducing nuclear dangers to both of us before the nuclear war starts." He said, "The way to save yourself and your family from being killed in a nuclear war is to keep such a war from happening. Once the missiles are launched, it is too late."

Those are obviously words of sanity and words of wisdom which must be taken to heart. However, the tone that's being taken by this new National Defense Strategy is completely contrary to that tone of sanity. And it is risking the escalation of just such a threat of thermonuclear war breaking out, either intentionally, or even accidentally.

In response to the Pentagon's new National Defense Strategy document and other recent developments, there have been protests from foreign ministry spokesmen in both Russia and China. The Chinese have released a statement, as you can see here on the screen, which is titled "China Blasts New U.S. Defense Strategy." This is what they had to say:

> If someone is always wearing dark glasses, they will never see a bright world. Peace and development are the themes of this era, and are also the shared aspirations of mankind. However, if some people look at the world through a Cold War, zero-sum game mindset, then they are destined to see only conflict and confrontation.
>
> We hope that the U.S. can align itself with the trend of the world and the will of the people, and put the world and China-U.S. relations into the perspective of cooperation.

So, that's a beautiful statement of exactly what we've been emphasizing. The year 2018 should be the end of geopolitics, and as the Chinese Foreign Ministry said, peace and development must be the themes of this new era—the shared aspirations of mankind. However,

White House/Shealah Craighead

President Trump (right) speaking with Russian Foreign Minister Sergey Lavrov in the Oval Office, May 10, 2017.

they said, as you can see, there are some people who continue to be involved in policymaking in the United States Administration, who "look at the world through a Cold War, zero-sum game mindset"; as opposed to what President Xi Jinping has proposed as a win-win paradigm of international relations.

The Russian Foreign Minister, Sergey Lavrov, also came out and denounced what he called the United States' "regrettable strategic policy towards Russia and China," which he said is one of "confrontational concepts and strategies." Here you can see on the screen the meeting between Secretary Lavrov and President Donald Trump. Helga Zepp-LaRouche said that what Sergey Lavrov has emphasized is that Russia does see that there is a division. President Trump himself is in favor of peaceful cooperation between the United States and Russia, and also between the United States and China; and he had repeatedly said that. "That it would be a good thing, not a bad thing," he says. But he notes that there is an insurgency against him from within the United States, directed from the British empire, which is preventing him from blocking these anti-Russia actions. Here's a quote from Foreign Minister Lavrov:

> When U.S. President Donald Trump received me in the White House, when he spoke with Russian President Vladimir Putin in Hamburg, and later they held telephone conversations, I did not see U.S. President Trump's charge [i.e.,

directive] for any sort of actions which could undermine his election campaign slogans that he wanted good relations with Russia.

Then he goes on to say that he sees that Trump's intentions are towards this good relationship with Russia, but that he's being forced into permitting anti-Russia decisions. He said, "However, we are comforted that recently, some members of the Congress, political circles in the United States, and some diplomats, acknowledge quietly in their confidential talks, the absolute abnormality of such a situation and the need to improve it."

So, there's a very clear recognition that there's a war going on inside this administration, inside the White House, and that President Trump is being backed into a corner against his intentions, to allow these sorts of anti-Russian and anti-Chinese positions.

This goes directly to the point, and it shows you that this persisting conflict within U.S. policymaking continues, and we are in an all-out battle for the existence of the Presidency.

Coup and Counter-Coup

I want to cite an article which was published by Stephen Cohen. He's a well-known Russian scholar, a professor at Princeton University. He stated this reality very directly in an article published in the *Nation* this weekend, titled—and I think this is very much to the point—"Democrats Are Repudiating FDR's Precedent of Détente with Russia"; and then the subtitle is "By criminalizing alleged contacts with the Kremlin and by demonizing Russia itself, today's Democrats are becoming a party of the new and more perilous Cold War." So, here are some quotes from what Stephen Cohen had to say:

The first of several détente policies [between the United States and Russia] was initiated by President Franklin D. Roosevelt in 1933, when he formally extended diplomatic recognition to the Soviet Union, then ruled by Stalin. That is, FDR was the father of détente, a circumstance forgotten or disregarded by many Democrats, especially today.

[T]oday, post Soviet Russia and the United States are in a new and even more dangerous Cold War, one provoked in no small measure by the Democratic Party and the still shadowy role of Obama's intelligence chiefs, not only those at the FBI, in instigating Russiagate allegations against Donald Trump early in 2016.

Russiagate allegations have been leveled by leading Democrats and their mainstream media against Trump every time he has tried to develop necessary cooperative agreements with Russian President Putin, characterizing those initiatives as disloyal to America, even "treasonous." Still more, the same Democratic actors have increasingly suggested that normal "contacts" with Russia at various levels—a practice traditionally encouraged by pro-détente U.S. leaders—are evidence of "collusion with the Kremlin."

[These allegations] are being codified into a Democratic Party program for escalated and indefinite Cold War against Russia, presumably to be a major plank in the party's appeal to voters in 2018 and 2020.

Consider instead the supremely existential and real danger of nuclear war, which as Reagan wisely concluded, "cannot be won and therefore must never be fought." And consider the false alarms of incoming nuclear missiles recently experienced in Hawaii and Japan. These episodes alone should compel any Democratic Party worthy of the name to support President Trump's pro-détente instincts and urge him to pursue with Putin agreements that would take all nuclear weapons off high alert But for that to happen, the Democratic Party would need to give American national security a higher priority than its obsession with Russiagate.

So, Stephen Cohen's citation of Franklin Roosevelt as the precedent for what the Democratic Party should be, and what the Democratic Party has lost in terms of the soul of the Democratic Party is, I think, very apropos. And obviously, Franklin Roosevelt's recognition that after World War II, we—out of necessity—needed to work together with Russia or the Soviet Union at that time, and China. Not only in defeating fascism, as we did accomplish in that great power relationship during World War II, but also in seeking to end the British Empire, and the kind of colonial policies that the British Empire had stood for, for over a century. And to bring peace through development to the entire world.

It's precisely for that reason that the LaRouche Political Action Committee has released its 2018 Party Platform. It's because the Democratic Party has been completely overtaken by these Russiagate fanatics, this neo-McCarthyism, who are intent on derailing any potential for U.S.A.-Russia-China cooperation. Here's what we said in the 2018 Policy Platform:

> We must end the coup against the President, and break the control over both parties, which adhere to the post-World War II geopolitical system which has produced decades of perpetual war and now threatens World War III by attacking China and Russia.

The Way Forward

That is a major aspect of this 2018 policy, this 2018 platform from LaRouche PAC. That's one of the aspects that we must absolutely escalate on and gain a flood of endorsements for this. It has to be seen as not politics, but as an existential threat to the United States if we are not be in collaboration and in dialogue with these two leading world powers—Russia and China. Those terrible experiences that the residents of Hawaii just went through, not to mention what the Japanese are now going through—those experiences should solidify in our minds and vividly bring to life that threat; that thermonuclear war is a very real danger and that this is a possibility which must be taken off the table if civilization is to survive.

Now, there is a very dramatic development on the front of breaking this "Russiagate" coup against President Trump. We don't have time to cover all of the aspects of this in detail, but let me quickly cite the actions by Congressman Devin Nunes. What he has done over the weekend could very well quickly bring this entire Robert Mueller Russiagate coup to its knees, and fully confirm the charges that were documented in the original LaRouche PAC pamphlet on the Robert Mueller operation. At the end of last week—and let me just go through a few details on this—while the rest of the country was being distracted by this melodrama over the government shutdown and the continuing resolution and so forth, Congressman Nunes wrote a four-page classified memo which documented—from sources at the FBI and the DoJ exactly what occurred around the original Steele report. Reports have been circulated that this discredited dossier, this so-called Steele dossier, was the basis for the FISA Court ruling allowing the FBI to spy on the Trump Presidential campaign. So this is not just a U.S. citizen under Section 702, but this is a

C-SPAN

Representative Matt Gaetz.

leading candidate for the United States Presidency, intelligence services under Obama's control spying on his enemies list. This is obviously in the league of what happened around Nixon and Watergate. Then, they continued this spying after the President took office.

On Thursday, the House Intelligence Committee voted along strict party lines—Republican versus Democrat; all the Republicans voted in favor of allowing every member of Congress to read the classified four-page memo from Devin Nunes. On Thursday night after that vote, a large number of Republican Congressmen took that liberty and went in to read that classified memo. They were shocked by what they saw, and they came out and went on national television and demanded that that memo be released to the public immediately. So, here are a few statements from some of the Congressmen who have read the memo.

The most extensive statement came from Congressman Matt Gaetz, who's a Republican from Florida. People might recognize Matt Gaetz as the Congressman who took to the floor, declaring that this operation against President was a "coup." So this is what Matt Gaetz said after having read the Nunes memo:

> The House must immediately make public the memo prepared by the Intelligence Committee regarding the FBI and the Department of Justice. The facts contained in this memo are jaw-dropping, and demand full transparency. There is no higher priority than the release of this information to preserve our democracy. I think that this will not end just with firings. I believe there are people who will go to jail. I was very persuaded by the evidence. You don't get to try to under-

mine our country, undermine our elections, and then simply get fired. So, I think that there will be criminal implications here. Why don't they want the American people to know the truth about what was going on with the government? How that impacted the President, his transition, his campaign. It just seems interesting to me that Democrats don't want us to know what the entire basis was in the first place for the Mueller probe. They want to drag this out through the mid-term elections to try to embarrass this President and distract this Congress from the crucial work we have to do to save this great country. Let's release the documents. The entire Mueller investigation is a lie built on a foundation of corruption. This will vindicate claims by many of us. It is a real attempt to undermine the President from the scariest of places. It would be ludicrous if we allow the Mueller probe to go ahead.

Then a number of other Congressmen who went in and read that Nunes memo, also came out and had some statements that were fairly short, but just as much to the point. Representative Jim Jordan from Ohio said, "What I read is as bad as I thought. Every American must see it to know what the FBI is up to." Congressman Scott Perry said, "You think about, 'Is this happening in America? Or is this the KGB?' That's how alarming it is." And Congressman Mark Meadows from North Carolina said, "It's troubling. It is shocking. Part of me wishes that I didn't read it, because I don't want to believe that those kinds of things could be happening in this country that I call home and love so much."

So, it makes you curious. What is in that memo, and will the Congress release that memo to the American people? Now the *Wall Street Journal* editorial board also came out and echoed exactly those same statements. It has a signed editorial under the title, "Transparency for Fusion and the FBI," and it calls for the release to the public of the House Intelligence Committee memo. It said the following: "The chance that Americans will learn what really happened between the FBI and Fusion GPS is growing, with Thursday's vote by the House Intelligence Committee to give every House member access to key information. Soon, the House should move to declassify all documents in the case that don't jeopardize intelligence sources and methods, so the public can get the complete story. The FBI played an extraordinary and trou-

bling role in the 2016 election, and access to the facts of what happened shouldn't be limited to FBI leakers, their media protectors, and partisans in Congress."

So, this is a very dramatic fight, and it goes directly along the lines of this fight over the existence of the U.S. Presidency. These seditious activities are intended to overthrow the duly elected President and, while he remains in office, to annihilate the potential for an end to geopolitics and a mutually beneficial relationship between the United States, Russia, and China. We see that there are high-level elements within his own administration who are going against that very intention, and are reinforcing this great-powers confrontation policy, this geopolitical agenda which led us into the Cold War and now could lead us to a hot war, World War III, which would be thermonuclear. We must take to heart what Helga Zepp-LaRouche has said: 2018 must be the end of geopolitics, or human civilization on this Earth very well might not survive.

So let me put our countdown on the screen one more time. There are eight days until President Trump's State of the Union address. It is coming up one week from tomorrow. Our campaign must be to put Lyndon LaRouche's Four Economic Laws on the agenda. That is, Glass-Steagall to erect a firewall between commercial banking and gambling on Wall Street; that entire bubble could blow out at any moment. We must instead return to national banking; what Alexander Hamilton originally instituted for this country. We must use that national banking capability to issue trillions of dollars in direct Federal credit for infrastructure and to uplift the skills and the technological level of the United States workforce, and to increase the productive powers of labor. And finally, that must all be included under a crash program for fusion power in the near term, and the expansion of manned space exploration. Secondly, this must all come within an end to geopolitics and a declaration that the United States is ending its policy of regime change, perpetual war, and competing economic blocs in a winner take all, zero-sum game strategy—and must instead join the New Silk Road and the paradigm of win-win cooperation that that represents.

So, we have eight days. We have a lot of work to do, and I hope that you will take the initiative to continue to escalate on this campaign and help us secure a victory.

Thank you very much for tuning in to larouchepac. com, and please stay tuned over the course of the coming week in what I'm sure will be a very dramatic eight days.

Hamiltonian Credit To Link the Americas to the Belt and Road

This is an edited transcript of Hal Cooper's address to the La-Rouche PAC Manhattan Project Dialogue, on Saturday, Jan. 13, 2018.

Hal Cooper: I would like to talk today about how we can rejuvenate our infrastructure and I'm going to talk about how we can connect the continents to New York, the nerve center of the United States, and connect Europe and Asia to North America.

Schiller Institute

Hal Cooper

We have the Silk Road program, and interestingly enough, in the very pro-establishment *New Yorker* magazine there's a big article this week about the Silk Road. Just to give you an example that it's becoming reality, within the last year the number of freight trains going between China and Europe on a round-trip basis, ending up in Duisburg, Germany, has increased from 3 a day to 25 a day. And that shows how much additional traffic

FIGURE 1

Eurasian Railway Network

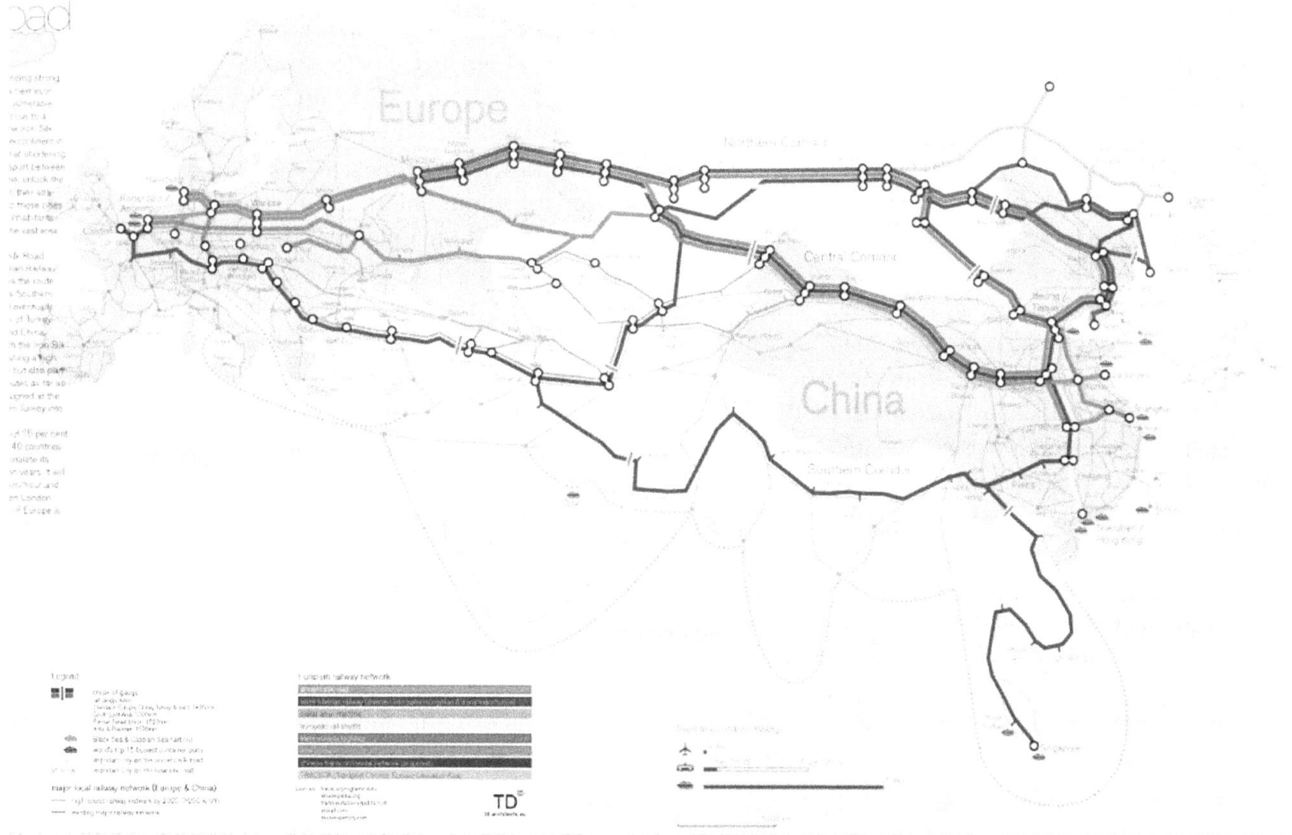

Proposed Intercontinental Connection Points for the Worldwide Railway Network

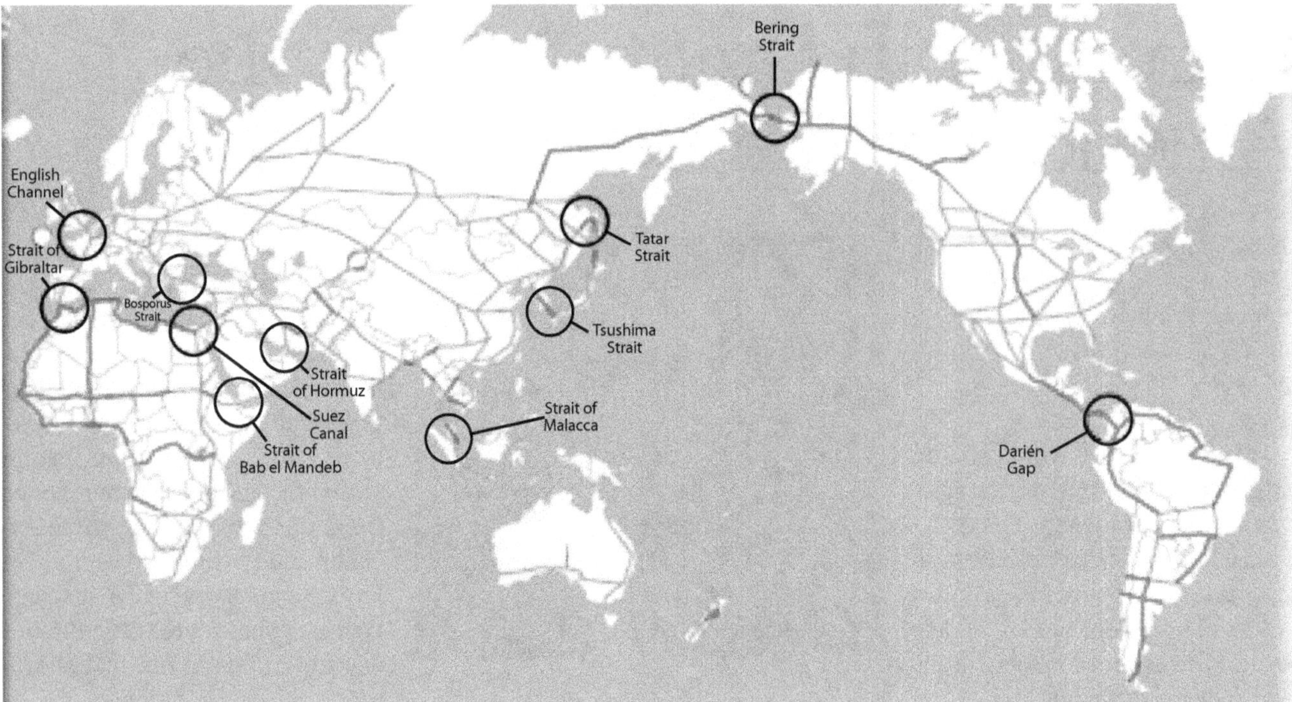

there's going to be, and that basically brings us more business and more economic activity, and more prosperity. China has very much taken the lead on this.

Unfortunately, we end up with more exports from China and more imports in Europe, and we need to balance that out, which means we need more manufacturing all over the world, including in Europe and especially here in the United States.

On this slide [**Fig. 1**], we see the Silk Road, the One Belt, One Road network as it is in Asia, and how it will be connecting to Africa, from a conjunction point on the rail line connecting Europe and Asia. There is already major investment in Asia from many of the countries—China and Russia in particular. One of these shown here is the Trans-Siberian Railway between Beijing and Moscow, where an almost 5,000-mile separate double-track electrified line is being built from Beijing to Moscow. This will make it possible to move freight and passengers between those two cities in two days or less, at speeds of up to 300 mph. Unfortunately, we are not doing this in the United States, and we're going to need to, if we want to ship things very quickly from point of origin to destination.

The Chinese high-speed rail system has over 10,000 miles of track now. Within five years it will be 15,000 miles of track, and rapidly building. The Chinese have

been utilizing an approach of building two parallel, electrified high-speed rail lines, one for passengers, one for freight, and later on in this presentation, I'll be talking more about that. That's a model we should be using in the United States. Unfortunately, our thinking on the subject of railroad building is not in a progressive mode.

In the United States, private freight railroads received the highest mark for infrastructure because they have basically maintained their infrastructure. The problem is, that it is very limited, and sufficient emphasis is not put on passenger service, because they basically don't want passenger service. It's very narrow thinking, which is based entirely on the idea of 90-day profits, rather than 50 year sustainability, which represents the difference in economic thinking between the United States and China.

The next slide [**Fig. 2**] shows the proposal for the world railway network. It would connect all the continents of the world together, particularly between North America and Asia, and that involves the critical infrastructure at the Bering Strait with the Bering Strait Tunnel, and of course a number of other major junction points in the world. In addition, we need to connect North America and South America together, and that means the Darién Gap between Panama and Colombia. China is now beginning to make major investments in

FIGURE 3

Proposed Bering Strait Railroad Tunnel and Natural Gas Pipeline Network

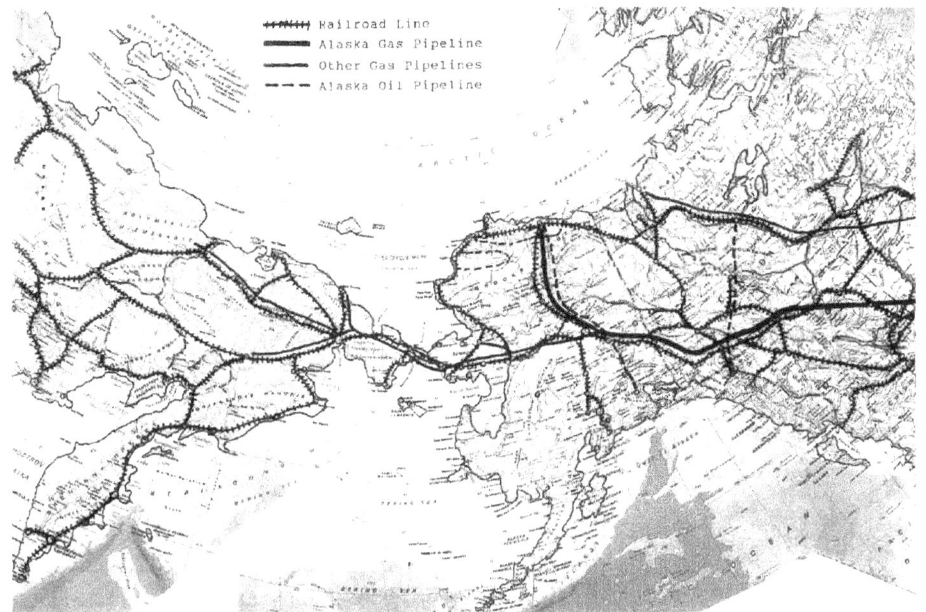

Central America and in South America, to bring that about. I think rather than trying to build a wall between the United States and Mexico, what we really need to be doing is developing the infrastructure to improve prosperity at the same time that we make an all-out war on the drug gangs and crime. We can't just have safety while doing nothing to improve the economic conditions of these countries. There has to be a major effort to redevelop and develop the economies, not only in the United States, but also in Mexico, Central America, and South America, all at the same time.

Linking Russia and the United States

This is the Bering Strait. [**Fig. 3**] We connect Alaska in the United States with Chukotka in Russia. I have been in both places. At the present time, western Alaska and Chukotka are devoid of a large population and there is not a lot of economic activity there. The thing that's missing is transportation. Now, there have been extensive studies done of connections to the Bering Strait Tunnel in Russia, but there's been virtually nothing done in the United States, with the exception of a feasibility study I did several years ago for the Canadian Arctic Railway, which sadly did not have the funds to go ahead with the project.

You can see these rail lines; you can see a loop around Alaska, and there are many resources there, oil and coal, and a number of minerals that need to be developed and exploited. The same is true for Russia. Rather than spending all this effort, as some of our various defense-oriented people are trying to do, and spending it all on the military, we should be doing what Russia is doing, which is promoting economic development in the Arctic region.

At its eastern terminus, the Bering Strait Tunnel would begin at Wales, Alaska. From there, it would progress to Little Diomede Island, which is on the United States side of the Bering Strait, and then to Big Diomede Island on the Russian side, with a four-mile separation between them, with trains going in and out of the tunnel.

The Bering Strait Tunnel proposal would be 53 miles under water, with the two islands in the middle. On the Chukotka (Russian) side you have the Tekhany Mountains, and on the Alaska side you have the Brooks Mountains, and you would need to have the tunnels extended so that the rail line on each side would extend beyond those mountains. And the water there is between 150 and 180 feet deep. It's in a zone of relatively stable geologic conditions. The volcanic activity and earthquakes are in the Aleutian Islands, several hundred miles to the south.

The One Belt, One Road, or Silk Road, extension from Asia into North America would need to come through the Bering Strait, and there would be a line across Alaska, and believe it or not, Alaska has already designated a 500-foot-wide corridor all across Alaska from Alcan in the east to Wales in the west—about 800 miles—which would be where the railroad would be located, connecting down to Anchorage. Then it would also need to go up to the areas along the North Slope, including where the Arctic National Wildlife Refuge is located. It would come down through the Yukon territory and British Columbia, through Alberta, Saskatchewan, and Manitoba. From there, rail lines would go through the northern tier of the United States and the northern Great Lakes region, and also across Ontario and Quebec, as far east as Montreal and Quebec City. Lines would come to New York, Boston, and Washing-

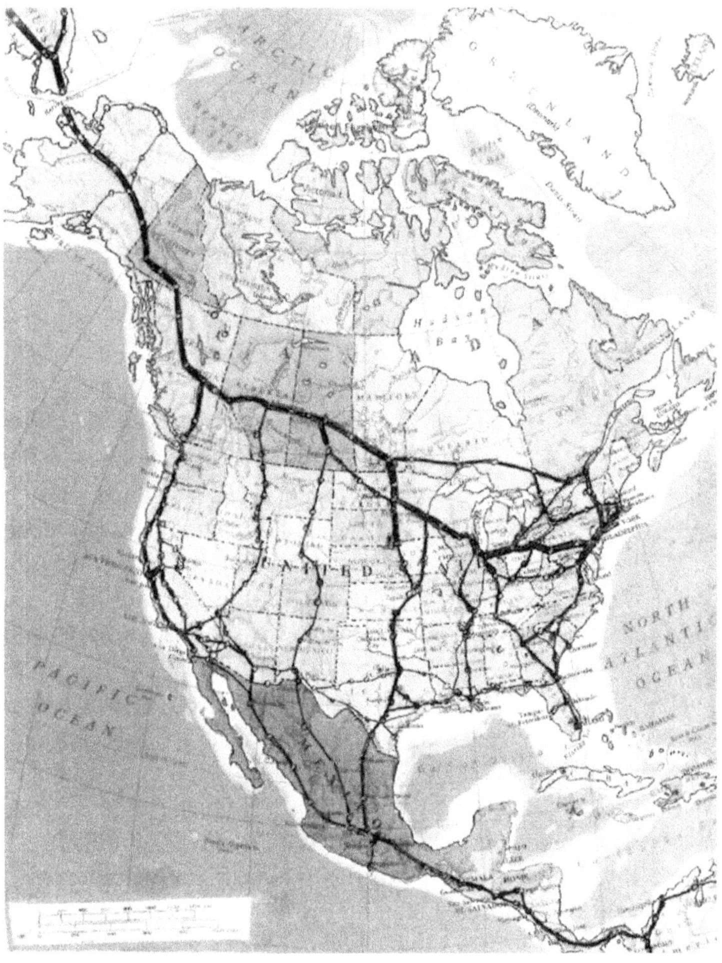

ton, by way of Chicago.

One of the key new developments is that the state of West Virginia has recently signed an agreement with the Shenhua coal company, the largest coal company in the world—it's a state-owned company in China—to develop the petrochemical industry, to improve and increase the natural gas production from the Marcella shale, to expand utilization of coal, and to make coal into chemicals, as well as for additional electric power generation. The Shenhua coal company has a subsidiary which develops, manufactures, and sells air pollution control equipment for coal-fired power plants. So they are way ahead of the United States in terms of the development of coal.

The next slide [**Fig. 4**] is an expanded view of the One Belt, One Road, and it's really focusing on what lines would need to be built through the United States, and how they would connect the southwestern United States with the One Belt, One Road, and also then go down through Mexico to Central America and from there to South America through the Darién Gap.

We need to do something besides having a drug economy. In fact it's reached the point in Mexico, where it's now very dangerous for Americans to go there because the level of crime and violence resulting from the propensity for drugs has just reached the point that it has created a very serious safety and law enforcement problem. We need to get that corrected, but we're not going to do it only on the basis of law enforcement. We've got to change the economies of those areas, and that means economic growth and development. The two best ways to make that happen are to build a railroad through there and then improve the electricity transmission and generation so that there is ability to have industrialization and development in Central America and in Mexico.

Water

In addition to rail and to roads, there is the issue of water, and there are areas of the United States that have too much water, and other areas that have too little. There is too much when we have a hurricane along the Gulf Coast, but, unfortunately, too little when we don't have enough water in California. We need to have a water distribution system that would start from the Mackenzie River in the Northwest Territories of Canada, and come down through the eastern part of British Columbia in the Rocky Mountain Trench, exactly as what the report by the LaRouche organization and the North American Water and Power Alliance (NAWAPA) plan showed. This is a report that has been suppressed. Water would come to California, and there would be no net loss out of the Columbia River. There would be water going east to the Courtenay River into the Missouri and then south. And believe it or not, the state of Arizona and the state of Nevada are looking at a new Interstate 11 Highway corridor going from Nogales, Arizona to Reno, Nevada, which could go through Tucson, Phoenix, and Las Vegas. This corridor would also have rail, water, and a freeway. So that shows that at least some thinking is going on.

The other major development project would be to build an irrigation canal going down through the Great Plains, because the Ogallala Aquifer—one of the largest in the world—is located there, and is running out of

Proposed Intercontinent High-Speed Rail Network

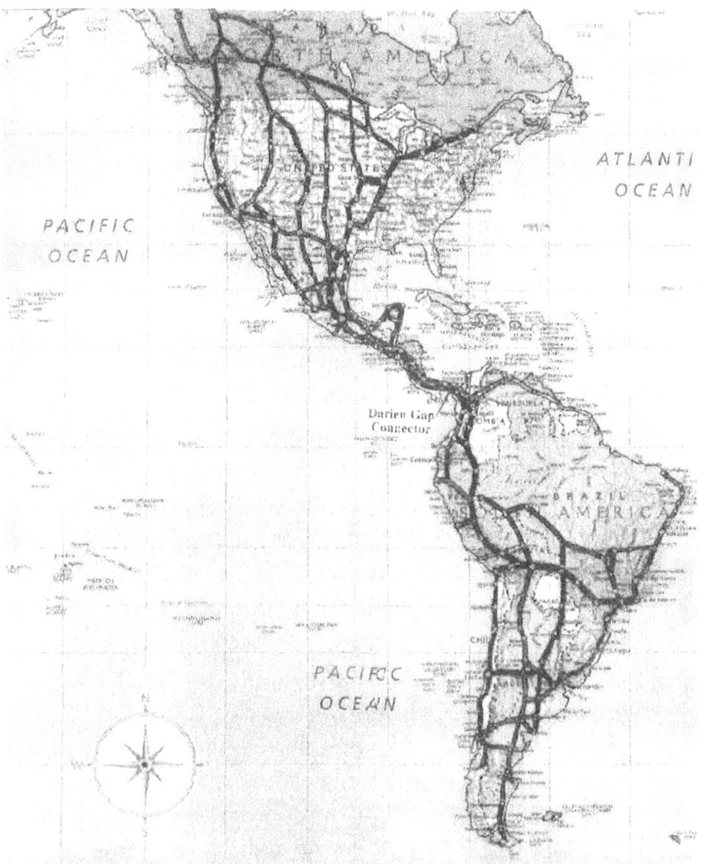

Proposed Route of the Darién Gap Railway Line

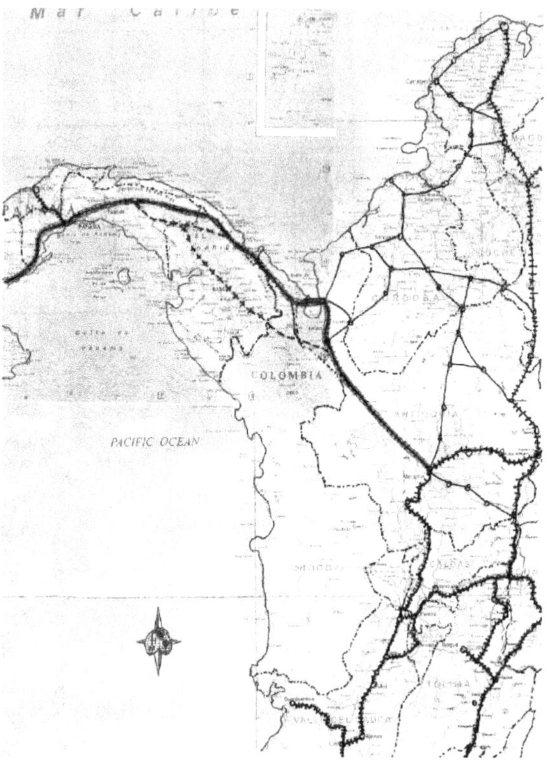

water. This is the biggest agricultural food-growing area of the United States, other than the San Joaquin Valley in California.

To go one step further, we need to be building facilities for the storage of water, and for water transport. We have areas of the United States which are getting too much rain—we've certainly seen that on the Gulf Coast, in Florida and Texas this year, but we have it in other places—and then we also see places such as in California and parts of the Western United States, including in some places in West Texas, where we don't have enough water. We should be collecting storm water and moving it around the country to where it's needed, and that means building lots of storage reservoirs as well as canals. I propose that these could be built along and underneath existing railroad lines, where we would have water transmission pipelines and perhaps even a magnetic levitation rail or hyper-loop tubes, should that technology ever be developed. We would have parallel, double track, electrified high-speed passenger and freight lines just exactly like what are being built and already in operation in China, and we need to follow

their model, and have these corridors specifically designated for transportation.

The *New Yorker* magazine this week has been forced to acknowledge the fact that the Silk Road is coming and that it should be coming to the United States. This is the model we should be following in terms of what we do. In Lanzhou, China is building a new city in parallel with the old one, so they can foster their economic growth and development. Here in the United States, instead of investing in productivity and development, we've invested in gambling and speculation: One brings us benefits, and the other doesn't bring us anything at all except trouble.

A Rail System for the Americas

Now, this is a proposed network for rail through both North America, Central America, and South America, with a connection at the Darién Gap. [**Fig. 5**] China is talking with Chile, Argentina, Brazil, and Peru. There's a bi-oceanic railroad being proposed between Santos in Brazil and Lima in Peru, going through Bolivia and Brazil and Peru, plus other rail systems as well.

This is where the Darién Gap would be, [**Fig. 6**] which would be the parallel to the Bering Strait, in completely opposite conditions, in tropical conditions

Proposed National High-Speed Rail System

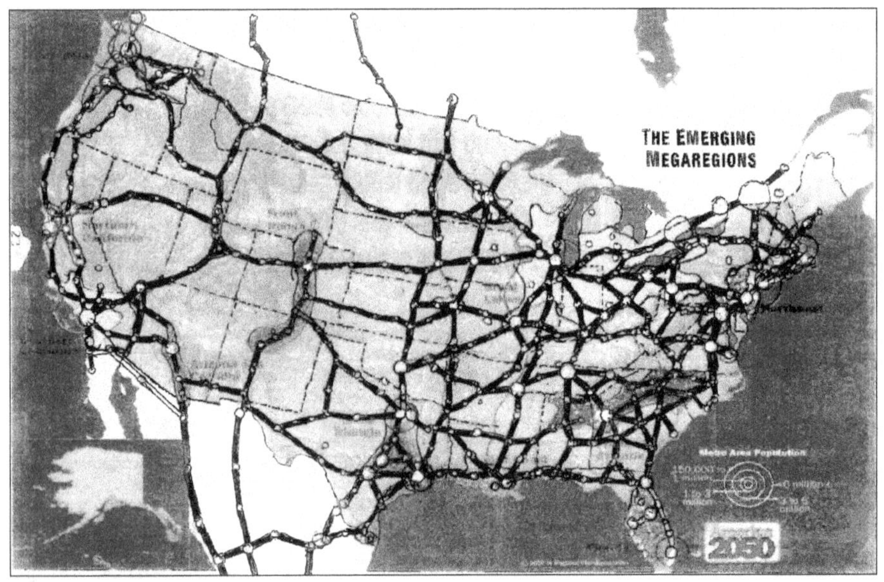

freight and passengers, and it should be done according to the same concept of the design that China is doing right now, and of course could become very much a component of the One Belt, One Road system.

One of the possibilities for this, is a proposal from a company here in the state of Washington—which owns some land—of rebuilding the old Milwaukee rail between Chicago and Seattle as a high-speed rail corridor for both passengers and freight, and it would go across the central part of the state of Washington, and it would connect Spokane and Seattle with Missoula, Bozeman, and Billings, and then go south with a connection into the Twin Cities [Minneapolis/St. Paul], and Milwaukee, and then to Chicago. Another route is the present Amtrak Cardinal route, going through West Virginia—which already has the beginnings of a major Chinese investment, much ahead of anything in the United States. This could be connected to the Northeast Corridor near Richmond, Virginia, and going all the way up to Washington and Philadelphia and New York, all the way to Boston. The Northeast Corridor is probably the most critical rail element in the United States.

where it's warm, versus where it's dry and cold up in the Bering Strait. You would need a 15-20 mile long bridge over the Gulf of Uraba, just inside Colombia. I would suggest building on the mountain range to the east so you didn't have to go through the swamp, although that route is a possibility as well, where the present highway is partially built. There's a critical section going from the far south in Panama, into northwestern Colombia, and there's opposition to building the road because they don't want this being used as a conduit for drug dealers.

This proposal would need to have governmental participation, and preferably as a part of the entirety of what is needed for Central America, aiming into South America.

That ends the One Belt, One Road part. Now, we're going to talk about New York.

The United States

In last Sunday's edition of the *New York Times Magazine*, they had an article called "The Case for the Subway," and why we should continue the subway, why we should fix it and take care of the many problems it has, which all of you know much better than I.

This is a map [**Fig. 7**] of a national high-speed rail system connecting the major urban regions of the United States, the Northeast, the Midwest, the Southeast, Florida, Texas, the Rocky Mountains, the Southwest in Arizona and New Mexico, California, and the Pacific Northwest. This would be needed for both

Coal

We need to reorient our coal-based generation, and rather than following the environmentalist mode of "let's get rid of coal and fossil fuels, and let's just have renewable energy," we need to actually think about capturing the rare-earth metals and precious metals, and base metals and strategic metals and other mineral resources that are in the coal, because it's Mother Nature's own activated carbon absorption system, and this should be done in conjunction with electric power generation, including reconstitution of some of the coal plants. Interestingly enough, a lot of the coal has quite a bit of uranium in it! And that would be a very good way of capturing that resource and using it for nuclear power plants, which we need to do more of, rather than trying to find ways to close them down.

Coal is one of the major resources of the United States, with large deposits located in the Rocky Mountains, in the Midwest, in Appalachia and in Texas, too.

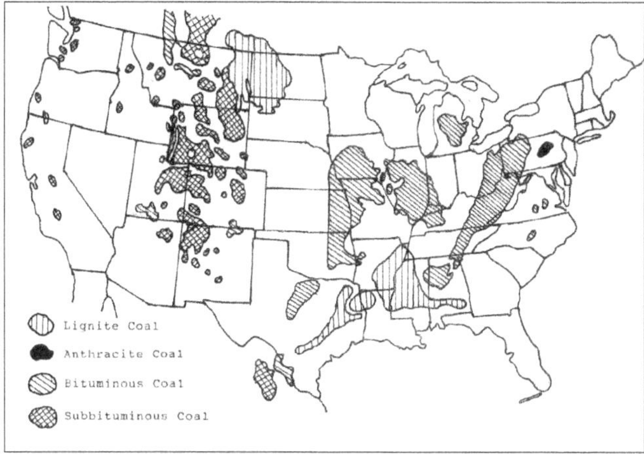

FIGURE 8
U.S. Major Coal Deposits by Type

FIGURE 9
New York City Area Major Commuter Railroad Lines

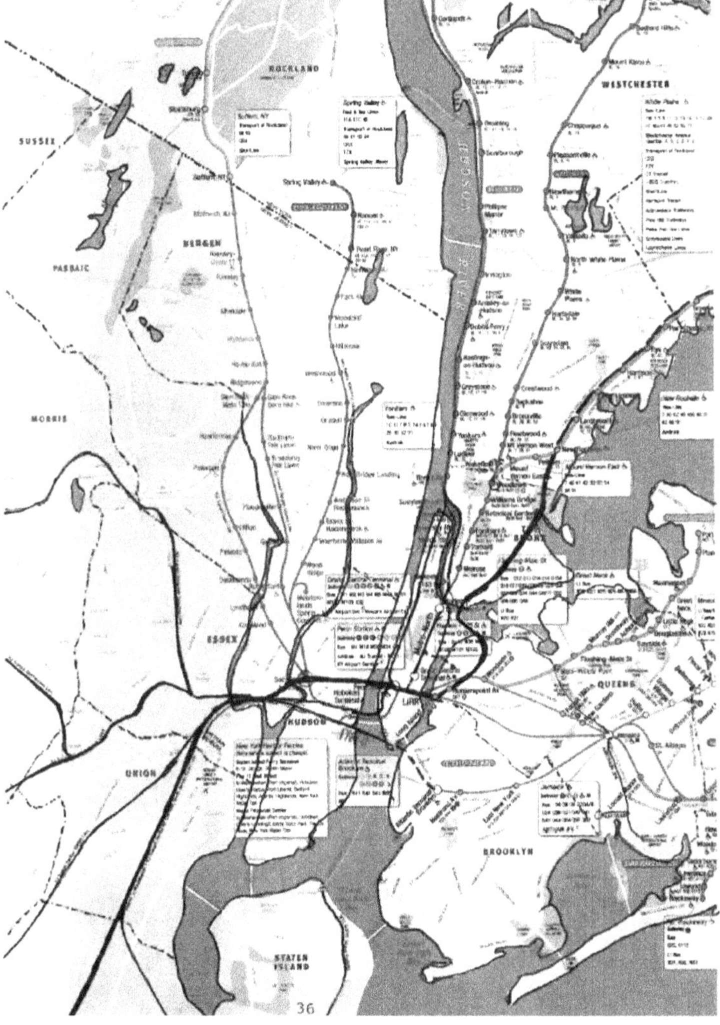

[**Fig. 8**] Because West Virginia has become the subject of this major investment by China, it certainly will become much more important, especially as it begins to grow economically. We would eliminate the economic depression conditions that were associated with the Obama Administration, and instead create much more the conditions for prosperity. Their goal is to greatly expand petrochemical production in that region, including from the Marcella shale, which in addition to coal comes into West Virginia.

New York

China now has 60% of the total distance of high-speed rail lines in the world within their country; and they're building more and more. They're going to be exporting to other countries. China has built a system where you have the passenger line, with the freight line right next to it. This gives you the ability to move very large numbers of trains very quickly between the cities, and that's something we need to follow China's lead on and it will take the efforts of China to support us.

At the opposite end of the pole, is the situation we have in New York with our subway system, and in contrast to the modern Chinese system, we now have a very decrepit system, because we lack development and maintenance.

The system that currently services New York consists of the existing subway system, the commuter rail lines, Amtrak and the PATH. These are all different systems, and in some cases they don't even connect. I'm proposing that we build a line from Hoboken to 14th Street on the west side of Manhattan up to Penn Station, for both subway trains and also for the inter-city trains, so we take some of the pressure off the line which is for the Gateway Project—which we badly need to have built—into Penn Station. Penn Station will need to be expanded. We also need to have a connection between Grand Central Station Terminal and Pennsylvania Station.

The subway system is the key growth factor in New York, and many other proposed expansions are needed. One of these is the 63rd Street East Side Access Project; another is a new PATH line from Lower Manhattan over to Brooklyn, so you have the ability to connect directly between Newark Airport and Kennedy Airport in New York. We need a rail connection between Brooklyn and Staten Island, from the Fort Hamilton area to Point Richmond in Staten Island; and then a series of additional routes for the subway, serving areas of New York City that are not covered now. In the meantime, we also have to immediately fix up the existing subway lines. We need to have a fix on where the problems are—including PATH and Amtrak—and what we need to do; and this all needs to be electrified if it's not already.

This is a view [**Fig. 9**] of the major rail lines coming into New York City from Connecticut, from Westchester, Duchess County, from Rockland and Orange Counties on the west side of the Hudson in New Jersey, and the Long Island Railroad, which is the most extensively used rail system in the United States. It has a significant electric demand, and the Consolidated Edison Company in particular might be hard-pressed to serve additional lines if they're built. Interestingly enough, when we look at the population projections of the New York Metropolitan Area, in the future they're going to be primarily in New Jersey and that means we're going to need more for more transit, serving more areas, farther and farther away from New York City. We're going to need to build them if we're going to maintain the prosperity of the city, which we must do. A number of new connections also need to be built: The Long Island Railroad, the Metro North Railroad, the New Jersey Transit, plus Amtrak.

This is a view [**Fig. 10**] of the trackage of the Metro North Railroad and the Long Island Railroad,

A J train leaving the Chambers Street station in Manhattan.

FIGURE 10

Metro-North Railroad

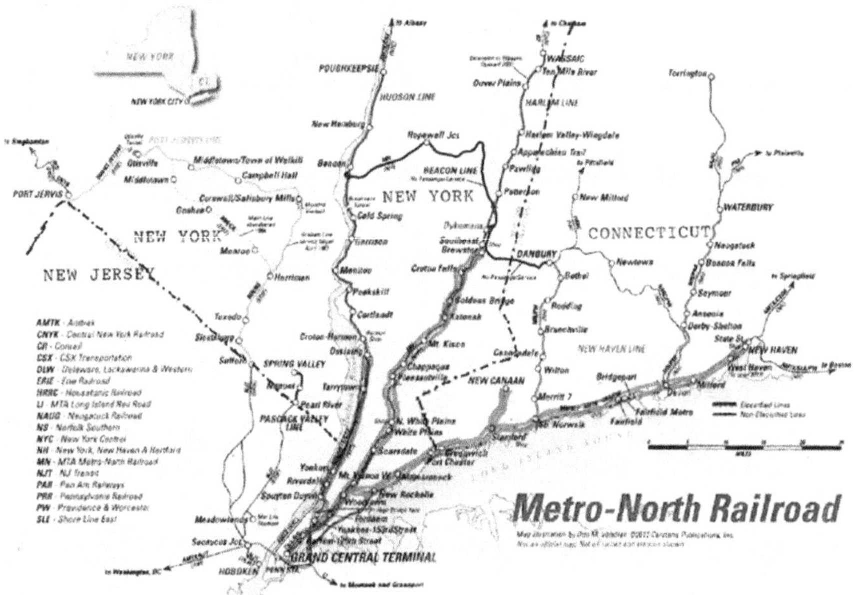

Long Island Railroad

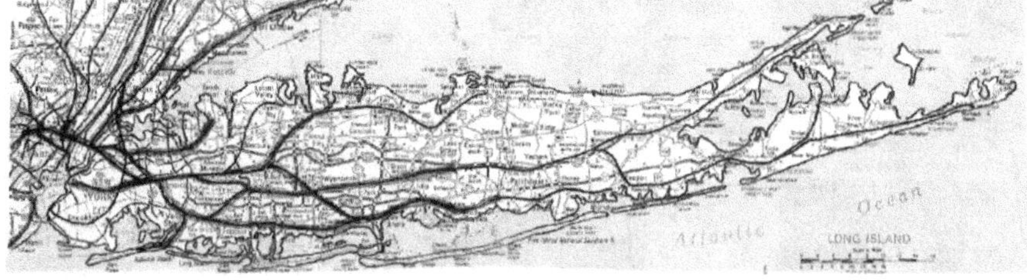

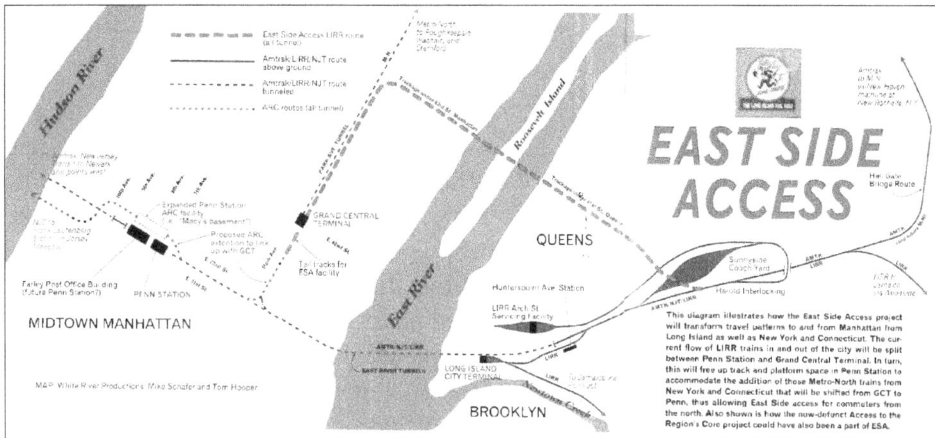

and the lines in red are electrified, and ones that are not are in black. We need to expand the electrification. Unfortunately we have up to seven different voltages, for different systems that are either third rail or overhead catenary. That all has a long historical basis, but we do need to unify, and put them all under the same technology, if we can.

We also have the East Side Access Project [**Fig. 11**] going from Sunnyside Yard in Queens into Grand Central and unfortunately, that's coming in at a cost of $3.5 billion a mile; whereas, by comparison, the Chinese are building their tunnels for $450 million a mile, and I think we'd better get the cost factors under control in New York.

The Gateway Project in New York would be connected to New Jersey, and this is one that so far the Trump Administration has not agreed to provide the financing for. They may be balking at the $29 billion cost—that works out to about $2.5 billion a mile— and it just doesn't seem like this is very realistic and needs to be reduced.

Under the Gateway Project, here is what the future would be. [**Fig. 12**] In addition, we need a series of loops to make it easier for existing train traffic to flow. Any future track configuration must be mostly four-track lines because they're going to handle lots of traffic. There's about 450 trains a day coming into Penn Station from the west and 700 a day coming in from the east. So there's a lot of traffic! And a lot of people are being moved—650,000 a day use Penn Station and 350,000 a day use Grand Central.

There is also the issue of freight traffic. We need to build a tunnel between Greenville Yard in Jersey City and Fort Hamilton, so that we can connect these, finally. The original proposal for that was in 1910, but it was never built. They built the tunnel into Manhattan for the passengers, but they never built the freight line. In the 1920s, Robert Moses stopped it all from being built. All the way back in 1895 they had a plan for building tunnels, both for passengers into Manhattan and freight

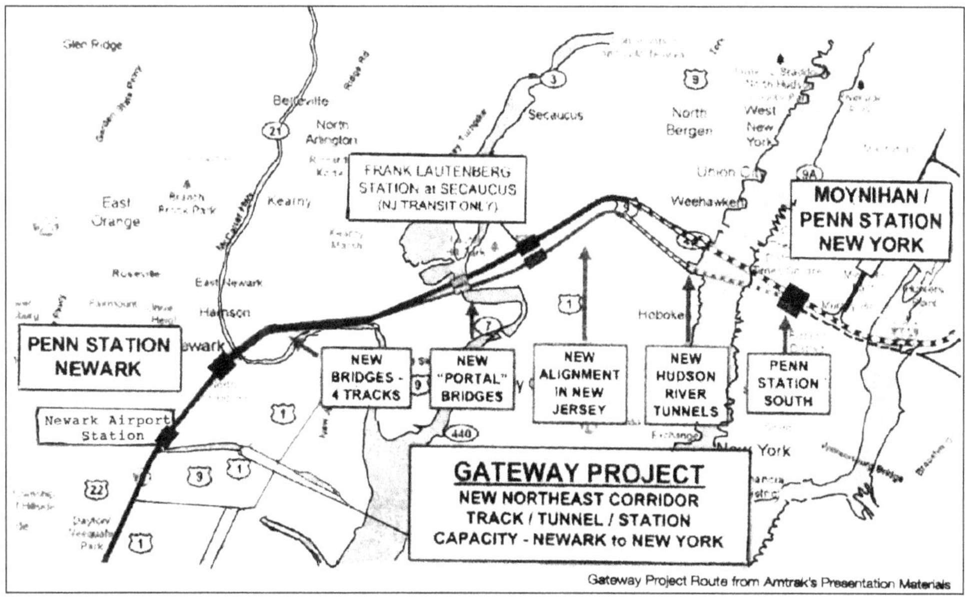

Existing Freight and Passenger Railroad Corridor Across the Northeast U.S.

into Brooklyn. They built the passenger part, but they never built the freight line.

Hamiltonian Credit

The Pennsylvania Railroad when it existed—it doesn't exist any more, it's been broken up into Conrail, CSX Norfolk Southern, and Amtrak owns the Northeast Corridor—was throughly electrified, beginning in 1928, up until 1932. The Pennsylvania Railroad financed this with its own bonds, but then it could no longer. When the Reconstruction Finance Corp. was created, their main project was a $200 million project to complete that electrification, financed through the RFC with a credit system, exactly as LaRouche has proposed today. The Reconstruction Finance Corp. needs to be

recreated, and my guess is the legislation that created it could still be there, but you have to set up a national infrastructure bank and this would be a good project to show how it would really work, because it did in the past. In World War I, the rail system broke down. The trains all had steam locomotives, and they all had to be serviced, and the logistics just broke down—there was tremendous difficulty getting traffic to the ports. Whereas, in World War II, once the electrification was completed, they were able to move lots of traffic of goods and people without any significant delays or major disruptions. It was very successful.

This [**Fig. 13**] is the Northeast Corridor, which is the most important single railroad and the most heavily used, and also overused, rail line in the United States. A lot of maintenance and upgrading must be done. We saw this in the problem with the bridge over the Hackensack River, getting stuck open. It happened the day before yesterday, as an example of the fact we need to do a lot, to fix it up.

A modernized and expanded rail system in the Northeast Corridor would get freight moving through the New York area, because right now it has to stop at the Hudson River and we need rail connections for that. We will also have to address the question of high-speed rail and the fact that our present Northeast Corridor is going to get overloaded and therefore we need to build an expansion onto that, and we also need to find where people can live far away, in affordable housing, and be able to get to business or work or pleasure, relatively easily. And we of course have the same problem in California, and here in the Pacific Northwest.

The LaRouche movement is really showing the way it has to be done to get these infrastructure programs underway. I think the example we have of the Reconstruction Finance Corp.'s support for the Pennsylvania Railroad electrification in the 1930s is a good way to start, in conjunction with a national infrastructure bank and the creation of a credit system.

Thank you. [applause]

Neocons and Neoliberals Are Driving for War

Helga Zepp-LaRouche's weekly Schiller Institute webcast of Jan. 18 can be seen at http://newparadigm.schillerinstitute.com

Harley Schlanger: Hello. I'm Harley Schlanger. Welcome to this week's webcast from the Schiller Institute, featuring the Founder of the Schiller Institutes, and President of the German Schiller Institute, Helga Zepp-LaRouche.

Helga, in just looking at the world in the past couple of days, it's clear there's been a worsening of the strategic situation. Much of this has to do with what you might call a neocon offensive, but it seems to be verging on a real crisis. And I want you to catch us up on that, to get started.

Helga Zepp-LaRouche: Yes. There were these hopeful signs about Korea, that the conflict could be solved in a detente manner, because North Korea and South Korea had many exchanges on the cultural front

Xinhua/Newsis

Ri Son-gwon (right), Chairman of the Committee for the Peaceful Reunification of the Fatherland of the Democratic People's Republic of Korea, shaking hands with South Korean Unification Minister Cho Myoung-gyon in the truce village, Panmunjom, Jan. 9, 2018.

around a joint delegation to the Winter Olympics in PyeongChang—also a joint women's ice hockey team—and, in general, the Red Cross is trying to bring families together again. This was all very promising. But now, unfortunately, the situation is being totally hyped up.

U.S. Department of State

U.S. Secretary of State Rex Tillerson, flanked by (left to right) Republic of Korea Foreign Minister Kang Kyung-wha, Canadian Foreign Minister Chrystia Freeland, and Japan Foreign Minister Taro Kono, at the beginning of the Korean Peninsula Summit in Vancouver, Canada, on Jan. 16, 2018.

There was a conference in Vancouver, Canada, to which the United States and Canada invited 24 ministers of all the countries which were allies of the United States in the 1950-53 Korean War, Countries such as Greece and Cyprus were invited, but not Russia and not China.

This was seen as an obvious effort to reinstitute a military alliance against Russia and China, which was met with very sharp criticism from these two countries. This comes in the context of North Korea's warning that the United States has started tunnel drills preparing an invasion, and is using the 82nd and 101st U.S. Airborne Divisions, which were used for the invasion of Iraq and Grenada.

There was also a very incisive article in the Chinese Global Times referring to this, which begins by saying that in terms of U.S.-Chinese relations, 2017 was much better than expected, because of the good understanding between President Xi and President Trump. They had three face-to-face meetings, and they've had many letters and telephone exchanges. However, the article points out that the difficulty is that we're not talking with the United States, but the "Divided States," referring to the total division between the pro-Trump and the anti-Trump people. It goes on to say that the United States is becoming increasingly uncomfortable with China, because China is becoming more confident and the United States is absolutely not used to that.

Then the article brings up the subject of trade war, because the GOP is expected to use the trade deficit issue in this year's election campaign. It also points out that North Korea has made such unexpected advances—referring to the fact that North Korea is now a nuclear power with ICBMs—that North Korea has crossed the red line for the United States, and that

U.S. Army/Staff Sgt. Sinthia Rosario

An M280 Multiple Launch Rocket System, assigned to the Republic of Korea/United States Combined Division, firing into the East Sea off South Korea, July 5, 2017.

the latter is preparing for a showdown this year. The article states it just like that.

The article also says that sanctions against China will not work, because half of the products exported from China into the United States, come from firms which are American firms.

And then at the very end, it says that the U.S. National Defense Authorization Act of 2018 includes the intention to strengthen military relations with Taiwan and have U.S.-Taiwan naval port-of-call exchanges. But it says when the first U.S. Navy aircraft carrier docks in Kaohsiung port in Taiwan, that will be the moment the People's Liberation Army will force the unification of China by military force.

So I find this quite worrisome. In addition, you had a false nuclear attack alarm in Hawaii, which we should talk about in a second, but that was also commented on by China's media, saying that this is a warning sign that there is obviously a full-fledged prepared plan for a military war with North Korea. And then three days later you had a missile false alarm in Japan.

I think these developments demonstrate that the situation is really very unstable. At this Vancouver meeting, Tillerson rejected the "double freeze" offer by Russia and China, and Trump as well. In an interview with Reuters, he said that maybe there is no peaceful solution for North Korea. I think that these are all warning words and signals.

Schlanger: There seems to be a bit of schizophrenia here, because at the same time that President Trump had a very positive discussion with President Xi Jinping, I think two days ago, in addition to the positive motion between South and North Korea—the South Korean President last week praised President Trump. However, at the same time, this growing chorus against China is emerging.

The *Economist* last December had a story about China's "sharp" power, and China "infiltrating" and "menacing" American universities, recruiting people through what? The Confucius Institutes, doing such subversive things as teaching Chinese to Americans. So there's definitely something afoot here. Helga, you mentioned the Hawaii situation. Do you have anything more on that?

Zepp-LaRouche: It's now well known that this alarm took place, reporting that nuclear missiles were in flight against Hawaii, and everybody started to look for shelter and call up their relatives, because they thought this was the last time they would be able to talk to them. It took 38 minutes for the message to get through that this was a false alarm.

Tulsi Gabbard, the Democratic Congresswoman from Hawaii, made a very important statement about that incident. She said that the idea that you could have an instant nuclear war is directly tied to the crisis in Korea, and she indicated that the only way to stop this crisis, is for the United States to stop the policy of regime change, because as long as Kim Jong-un is convinced that the only way for North Korea to avoid the same fate as Saddam Hussein and Qaddafi is for North Korea to be a full-fledged nuclear power, this problem will continue. So she demanded an immediate end to this regime-change policy.

And I already mentioned that the *Global Times* article said that this is a signal that there are already full-fledged war preparations for a U.S. military conflict with North Korea, which obviously could easily get out of hand. This article also mentions, by the way, that the U.S. forces are on high alert all the time, and you only have minutes to stop the crisis, or it could get out of control.

I think we are in a very, very difficult and very dangerous moment again.

Schlanger: Another part of that dangerous moment is the discussion of a new U.S. strategy towards Syria. After both President Trump and Secretary of State Tillerson said the U.S. policy is not regime change, it appears as though they're again

Xinhua

Turkish army tanks take part in offensive to oust Kurdish militia from Afrin, Syria, on Jan. 22, 2018.

bringing up the the idea that Assad must go. Why is that happening now?

Zepp-LaRouche: There seems to be a reassertion of neocon policy in the Trump Administration, because, as you said, it had previously been said many times that the focus is no longer on Assad. But now Tillerson, in a speech at Stanford University's Hoover Institution, spoke about a new Syrian strategy. He said it was a mistake for the United States to prematurely leave Iraq in 2011, and we will not make this mistake again. The U.S. will stay there [in Syria] for an indefinite period of time, until ISIS is completely defeated. He also said that the United States insists on Assad's eventual departure.

This is unacceptable! Syria is a sovereign government, and this is basically a precursor for a new crisis around Syria.

In addition, there is a new military conflict: [Turkish President Recep Tayyip] Erdogan and some other politicians in Turkey have accused the United States of militarily supporting a group of Kurds which the Turkish government calls terrorists, because there are certain members of the Turkish opposition PKK involved. There are already Turkish tanks and troops being deployed right now. Erdogan said that this is a plan to divide Syria. Another spokesman said this is a plan to divide NATO, because this is unacceptable for Turkey, which is a member of NATO.

This escalation is similar to what you see in the North Korea crisis, and I think it is directly connected to the incessant drive for a coup against Trump in the United States. It sometimes seems that he is being surrounded by such people. Trump's policy was—and that has been acknowledged by Putin and Chinese President Xi Jinping—to improve the relationship with Russia and China, but there are these vacillations which are very, very worrisome.

Schlanger: Some of the attacks on China and Russia—on their press arms, such as *RT* and *Global Times*—are coming from the National Endowment for Democracy, which has also been very much involved in the coup against Ukraine. There is also the Hoover Institution, as you mentioned. So, it's the same old networks, and these are the people Trump ran against in his Presidential campaign.

You mentioned the Mueller investigation: Do you think this is a major part of the resurgence of the neocons, trying to pin Trump down and keep him totally tied up with this investigation?

Zepp-LaRouche: Yes. The British newspaper, the *Spectator*, reported one year ago that these forces will not stop trying to neutralize Trump, either by carrying out a coup, by impeachment, or by assassination. One option is to pin Trump down so that he capitulates to these neocon policies, and get him "reined in" as they say, into the existing trans-Atlantic geopolitical policy. I don't think that is the end of the whole story, but I think the coup forces are clearly not yet defeated. I find it quite remarkable that somebody who doesn't like Trump at all—Ray McGovern, from the Veteran Intelligence Professionals for Sanity (VIPS)—said that this is a *clear coup* that the FBI is involved in. Only somebody who is completely blind will not see that it's a coup involving British intelligence against the sovereign government of the United States.

There is now a growing number of congressmen who are demanding prosecution against Obama's director of national intelligence, James Clapper, for his role in all of this, and the ongoing hearings in the Congress may lead to indictments, or to a special prosecutor against the people who are doing this—so it's not yet decided.

But I think we must stay alert.

How Can You Be So Optimistic?

Schlanger: Clapper has also been saying that Russia and China have been attacking the "very fundamental underpinnings of our democracy." So he's someone who's very much involved.

James Clapper, the Obama Administration's Director of National Intelligence.

And on this same note, I just picked up a story today, reporting that a spokesman for Barack Obama said that Obama is going to play a prominent role in the 2018 elections. Now, in some ways, he never left, because hasn't he been one of the people coordinating the whole Russiagate story?

Zepp-LaRouche: Yes, he moved into a house in Washington, to practically be the leader of this "resist" movement. And I think people have forgotten, that the danger now is that Trump may fall back into the same policies which were absolutely characteristic of the Obama Administration in respect to the escalation in Syria and similar types of operations. People should remember that it was Obama who launched all illegal drone attacks. This is very worrisome, because the problem now is that it appears that no one in the United States is capable of implementing the kinds of policies which we are campaigning for very hard—the immediate ending of the danger of a financial crash through reinstatement of Glass-Steagall, and the Four Laws which my husband designed several years ago. This is really an appeal to our viewers to refer to us, because I think that what is lacking right now is a positive leadership for the United States.

Schlanger: It's not a coincidence that this new escalation is occurring as the warning signs of the popping of a new financial bubble have emerged, and this is having a profound effect in the United States, because we have a possible government shutdown coming up. They're playing games with that—but these are all diversions. The real issue is, why are we still tolerating the Bush-Obama policy of protecting Wall Street and destroying the physical economy? That's the basis for the mobilization around the Four Laws.

If you could just say a little bit more about that, because we do have our organizing teams on Capitol Hill, we have a new pamphlet on LaRouche's Four Laws, and this is the unique solution to this crisis.

Zepp-LaRouche: Right now, we're at the beginning of the explosion of the corporate debt bubble. There is Carillion, a huge firm in Great Britain which is folding up; and then you have the Steinhoff Group in South Africa which is near collapse, with ramifications for many major banks, which have had significant losses; that is all related to the fact that the corporate debt bubble is much, much worse today than in 2008. And the situation is simply much worse in terms of all the parameters than 2008.

The very interesting author, Nomi Prins, who used to be a high-ranking manager in Goldman Sachs, has written her sixth book [*Collusion: How Central Banks Rigged the World*, May 2018]. There is a preview available—the book will come out in May—in which she describes how as a real insider, she worked for Goldman Sachs for 15 years, and as she was climbing up the career ladder, she came to know how criminal the activities were on the higher level of this bank, as well as all the others. She decided to no longer pursue that career, and instead to become part of the solution. So she is a whistleblower so to speak, and she describes how, after 2007-2008, the Federal Reserve and the other central banks, by issuing zero interest rate money, and turning on the liquidity pump, have pumped $16 trillion into the system just since 2007 and 2010. And as you know, this is still going on to the present day.

That money did not go into investment in the real economy. Instead, that essentially *gratis* money, money at absolutely no cost, was used by the big banks and big corporations in large part to buy back their own stocks. This of course increased the profit of these people by incredible margins. As a result, they became richer and richer; but the corporate debt bubble also became bigger. And this is now threatening to explode again.

Anything could trigger that collapse. We are sitting on a powder keg, and as you said, I think there *is* a direct connection between the worsening of the financial crisis, and the willingness of these same people to go for military adventures which could lead to World War III. This geopolitical faction does not want to see a situ-

creative commons

The New York Stock Exchange on Wall Street, New York City.

ation where China and the Belt and Road Initiative are growing; the Chinese economy is doing well and all the countries which are cooperating with China are doing well, while their own system is collapsing. So I think there is an *immediate* connection between the danger of a new financial crash, and the military escalation.

That makes our own global intervention very important, for our colleagues in the United States in particular. They are deployed to go to the Congress. They have many meetings in both Houses of the Congress. They are deployed to go to the state capitals, and they have many meetings there. We have produced a brochure going through the need for the implementation of these Four Laws and why the United States must join with the New Silk Road in a new paradigm.

That mobilization is really important, and the good thing is that we are finding more and more people who are really trying to understand the principles involved. Why Glass-Steagall is absolutely urgent? Why do you need to go back to a Hamiltonian National Bank and a credit system? Why do you need a crash program in space exploration and fusion technology in order to increase the productivity of the economy? People are trying to understand these concepts and show more seriousness, and of course we hope that this will also influence the surroundings of the State of the Union address, which Trump will give on Jan. 30. We need a mass mobilization of people to urge their Representatives and their Senators to do this.

Because, as you know, the problem is that the Democrats are generally not far from Wall Street, and neither are the neocons in the GOP, so it requires a very strong mobilization from the base of the population.

Schlanger: And just a couple of figures to amplify what you were saying: In the last five years, corporations have added $4.5 trillion to their debt, so it's now over $14 trillion. And of that, $2.7 trillion was used to buy their own stocks! So more than half of the lending to corporations went directly into stock purchases, and that's why the stock market is up—and that's why it's a bubble.

I'd like to pose a simple question to you—it's not really that simple, but—in the face of all this insanity, you've remained a fount of optimism, and a lot of people communicate with me, asking: "What is it that you guys know, that we don't, that we pessimists don't know?" I think this is an important point, because we were talking, before the program, about the Chinese intervention into Latin America and in Africa. There's so much going on that Americans don't know about—but where does this optimism come from?

Zepp-LaRouche: It comes from several sources. Let me first talk about the objective one, and then I'll come to the subjective one.

Objectively, when you look at the world from the top, so to speak,—I mean, you don't look at it from inside Germany, or inside the United States, or some other country—but look at it from the overall historical process which is unfolding right now. Then you see the clear division. In the trans-Atlantic world, there are people who generally expect that the future will be worse, that the coming generations will be worse off than they are, and that is a foregone conclusion. After all, they are told that the resources are limited, that you have to have restraint and conservation, and all of this kind of ideology. And look at the social injustices, the rate of poverty in the United States and in Europe— even in Germany, every sixth child is poor. There is an unbelievable situation in countries like Italy and Spain, and in Greece, where you have youth unemployment of 50-60%. So people have a grim perspective on the future.

cc:flickr.com/photos/eppofficial/

Pensioners demonstrate against austerity in Greece.

In large part, the politicians have absolutely nothing to offer as a vision for the future. The best example for that right now, is the never-ending coalition talks in Germany, which have already been going on for more than four months since the election. *None* of the parties has said one single word about what the future of Germany should be. Where should the world be? So people generally are desperate, they're frustrated, they think things are getting worse—and then they see all these calamities in the world, and they say, "I can't even look at the news any more—it's all terrible."

But that is only half of the truth, or less than half of the truth. Because if you look at the world from the standpoint of China, you see a completely different vector of developments. First of all, China has undergone the most incredible development. They have lifted 800 million people out of poverty over 20 years! They want to eradicate poverty by the year 2020, *entirely.* They are doing wonderful things in Africa, in Latin America, in other Asian countries, and even some European countries, so there is a sense of confidence; there is a sense that there *is* a future. And then, Xi Jinping at the recent 19th National Congress of the Communist Party of China, laid out his vision for where China should be in 2020, in 2035, and 2050. He laid out an incredible vision that by that time, China should be a fully modern, strong, socialist country, where the people are living happy lives: It should be culturally advanced, and scientifically strong, and people should have happier lives, not only in China, but around the world.

We know that the economic underpinning of that vision is progressing with the Belt and Road Initiative, building infrastructure, R&D centers, industrial parks, energy distribution, and production. This is all a realistic perspective, but it has a cultural dimension to it: They want to have a space Silk Road, and a cultural Silk Road. These are all initiatives which have given the Chinese people a tremendous sense of confidence, and that is a spark which has spread, so to speak, to the other countries which are participating in the Belt and Road Initiative.

As I stated at the beginning, China's warnings for this year with respect to the crises in North Korea, Taiwan, and similar situations, are very stark. These warnings show that China is not naïve, and is willing to react to defend its interests. So it's not all rosy and lacking a realistic view. However, the way they go about it, is absolutely one of optimism.

I also think that most people in Russia have the same attitude: This is why the popularity of Putin is at the high level of over 80% right now, despite the difficulties of the sanctions and so forth. I think the difference is that if you have a mission and a vision for the future, then you are optimistic, because it is in your own will and power to realize those visions.

So I think there is a clear division in the world population on this issue.

Now, I wanted to say something about the subjective reasons why, despite all of these dangers, I'm fundamentally very optimistic: The reason is that there is no point in worrying. You have to have a vision of how you want to use your life to contribute to the improvement of the human species. I have a vision which is not exactly the same as that of Xi Jinping, but my vision is also very much like that of my husband, with whom I've been working on this for more than 40 years—that we have a world where every human being on this planet can have a decent life, can have fulfillment of all of the potentialities that each person has—and that mankind can become adult, that we go back to the values which are characteristic of the American Revolution, of the German Classical period, of the Italian Renaissance, and other high points of culture. I'm optimistic that we can retrieve these qualities by having a cultural Renaissance of Clas-

Photo/China Daily

A teacher introduces a model of a spaceship to students on China Space Day, April 24, 2017, at the Science and Technology Children's Palace of Baotou, which launched a series of activities to promote children's interest in space science.

sical music, and Classical poetry. Since China is on that road already, by reviving the Confucian tradition, and by placing a lot of emphasis on Classical culture and on scientific breakthroughs, I think that the West should just re-think what our contributions to the advancement of universal history have been, and then revive them, and have a Dialogue of Cultures among the best traditions of all countries.

I think this is the human nature. I don't think the idea of geopolitics. or ravings or rantings like those we hear from Ted Cruz right now, are what make us human. I think we should *not* regard other cultures as an enemy by definition. China has reached out and said, "Let's join for a shared future of mankind. We are a community of destiny," and I think this idea of a joint humanity, of one mankind, is what we have to accomplish if we want to exist as a human species. But I think it is part of human nature that once you have the will and a good plan, and many people work together for the good plan, you can succeed.

Schlanger: I would recommend to our viewers, that this Winter, instead of catching the flu, people catch the Silk Road Spirit.

Helga, that brings us to a close. Thank you very much, and we'll see you next week!

Zepp-LaRouche: Good-bye.

The Promise of the Space Program To End Poverty Worldwide

The following is an edited version of a presentation given by Dennis Speed to the LaRouche PAC Manhattan Dialogue on Jan. 20, 2018.

We are going to take up a matter today, as a form of repentance for what we all should have realized last week. In the words of Malcolm X, "You've been had! You've been 'took'! You've been bamboozled." That's what happened last week to the country. The country accepted a liar, Illinois Senator Dick Durbin, as a truth-teller. *People accepted it* because—as many people said at the time—"I already knew that he thought that," about Donald Trump. So they presumed that Trump had said what the known liar, Durbin, claimed he said, even though the President stated that he had not said it.

This *prejudgment*, of course, is a practice that is not limited to the Presidency and this current President. It's one that people engage in all too often, and has caused great harm. But it can be corrected by simply admitting when you've been bamboozled. We ourselves, for example, failed to immediately check our own documents and to check the source of the statement being made. It turned out that we have a whole set of articles, set of statements, archived from the *Congressional Record* that told us exactly what was actually going on. So, in the future, what we can certainly say to anyone who is concerned about any future attack against the President of the United States, the first thing to do is to check that attacker's LaRouche file. *Whenever anybody attacks*

Donald Trump, the first thing that should be done is to check where that person stands on Lyndon LaRouche; check the file before you believe anything that is being said in any way. Check the LaRouche file.

Now, this is an important thing to say, because what we're going to try to do today is to introduce an idea, by means of not merely asserting that it's true, but by instead suggesting that there are things that you already know, which should have caused you to realize that this *idea* was true, long before this presentation was given. The reason for doing that, is that, in this way, we can quickly correct a problem that plagues the American people.

The space program, and the offer for the reintroduction of the space program put forward by President Donald Trump, is the natural point of unity for the human race, and particularly for the nations of Russia, China, and India, with the United States. Japan and others are, of course, also included. This is something

EIRNS/Dennis Speed

A rocket at the Kennedy Space Center, Cape Canaveral, Florida.

that John Kennedy famously talked about at American University, Washington, D.C. back in June, 1963 (see box). The nature of why there is a space program, or how it became policy, is the first thing we want to establish, because of the nature of the topic and what the topic is, fundamentally. It's what's contained in Lyndon LaRouche's book, *Earth's Next Fifty Years*. Today what I want to do, is simply talk about something that is now under discussion and is rather controversial inside of NASA.

John F. Kennedy at American University, June 1963

President Kennedy gave the speech excerpted here on June 10, 1963. The next day, June 11, he delivered "The Report to the American People on Civil Rights," in which he proposed the laws that would ultimately become the Civil Rights Act of 1963. To support that Civil Rights Act, Martin Luther King, with the assistance of Rev. C.L. Franklin, organized 125,000 people to march in the streets of Detroit eleven days later, culminating in King's speech at Cobo Hall before 25,000 people called "The American Dream." The Reuther brothers and the United Auto Workers joined with King, A. Phillip Randolph and others to organize the "March for Jobs and Freedom" in Washington, D.C. Excerpts of President Kennedy's June 10 speech follow.

… I have, therefore, chosen this time and this place to discuss a topic on which ignorance too often abounds and the truth is too rarely perceived yet it is the most important topic on earth: world peace.

What kind of peace do I mean? What kind of peace do we seek? Not a *Pax Americana* enforced on the world by American weapons of war. Not the peace of the grave or the security of the slave. I am talking about genuine peace, the kind of peace that makes life on Earth worth living, the kind that enables men and nations to grow, and to hope and to build a better life for their children not merely peace for Americans but peace for all men and women not merely peace in our time but peace for all time.

I speak of peace because of the new face of war. Total war makes no sense in an age when great powers can maintain large and relatively invulnerable nuclear forces and refuse to surrender without resort to those forces. It makes no sense in an age when a single nuclear weapon contains almost ten times the explosive force delivered by all of the Allied air forces in the Second World War. It makes no sense in an age when the deadly poisons produced by a nuclear exchange would be carried by wind and water and soil and seed to the far corners of the globe and to generations yet unborn.

Today the expenditure of billions of dollars every year on weapons acquired for the purpose of making sure we never need to use them is essential to keeping the peace. But surely the acquisition of such idle stockpiles which can only destroy and never create is not the only, much less the most efficient, means of assuring peace.

I speak of peace, therefore, as the necessary rational end of rational men. I realize that the pursuit of peace is not as dramatic as the pursuit of war and frequently the words of the pursuer fall on deaf ears. But we have no more urgent task.

Some say that it is useless to speak of world peace or world law or world disarmament—and that it will be useless until the leaders of the Soviet Union adopt a more enlightened attitude. I hope they do. I believe we can help them do it. But I also believe that we must re-examine our own attitude as individuals and as a Nation for our attitude is as essential as theirs. And every graduate of this school, every thoughtful citizen who despairs of war and wishes to bring peace, should begin by looking inward by examining his own attitude toward the possibilities of peace, toward the Soviet Union, toward the course of the cold war and toward freedom and peace here at home.

First: Let us examine our attitude toward peace itself. Too many of us think it is impossible. Too many think it unreal. But that is a dangerous, defeatist belief. It leads to the conclusion that war is inevitable that mankind is doomed that we are gripped by forces we cannot control.

We need not accept that view. Our problems are manmade therefore, they can be solved by man. And man can be as big as he wants. No problem of human destiny is beyond human beings. Man's reason and spirit have often solved the seemingly unsolvable and we believe they can do it again.…

NASA, the TVA, and Martin Luther King

In a conference that took place at Huntsville, Alabama last March, the subject was the relationship between NASA and the civil rights movement. It was called "NASA in the 'Long' Civil Rights Movement." One of our associates, Marsha Freeman, was at that conference. One of the things that she spoke about was that several of the people who are the official historians of NASA take issue with the fact that NASA did have a *social agenda*. As a Federal program located primarily in the South, in, for example, Langley, Virginia, or in Florida, where there were more lynchings going on in the United States than any other state in the Union, or in Texas, or in Huntsville, Alabama, or also in Louisiana and Mississippi, NASA, which is a science agency, had no choice and had, essentially, the inclination that it must, in fact, refute racial categorizations and anything other than the idea that the excellence of the operative employed for the space program is what qualified that person to participate in science and in frontier human endeavor. This was not new with NASA, and even in the case of the recent film, "Hidden Figures," and the book version that was also published, was a bit misleading, since the focus there was on the Gemini program, and John Glenn, and related figures, and that left out the fact that it was during the Second World War that the main changes actually began to occur, particularly in Virginia, in the employment of African-Americans in engineering and other scientific roles.

I want to quote something from what Marsha Freeman presented on that occasion last year. This was about President Franklin Roosevelt. She said:

> Even before his inauguration, just weeks after he was elected, President-elect Roosevelt toured the Tennessee Valley. The President saw that the conditions of life in the Valley were most akin to conditions in the Third World. The most backward regions of the nation, encompassing all of Tennessee and parts of Mississippi, Alabama, North Carolina, Kentucky, Virginia, and Georgia, had suffered conditions of extreme poverty for decades, poverty which had only been magnified by the Great Depression. *Just 37 days after taking office*, President Roosevelt transmitted a message to Congress to request "legislation to create a Tennessee Valley Authority." On May

Evening Star/Bernie Boston

Rev. James Bevel (second from right) and George H.W. Bush (left) at the Resurrection City encampment on the National Mall in Washington D.C. on May 22, 1968.

18, with his signature, the bill became law. In his request, the President outlined the specific goals of the new institution, including power development, flood control, reforestation, and agricultural restoration. But he continued that the power development plan begun during the First World War "leads logically to national planning for a complete river watershed involving many states, and the future lives and welfare of millions."

There's a reason that I particularly emphasize Marsha's citing of the Tennessee Valley Authority. People have heard about Martin Luther King and the Birmingham Children's March. The Birmingham Children's March occurred over the period from approximately May 1-2, 1963, through May 10-11. King had earlier gone to jail in Birmingham, because he had defied the Federal injunction which Bobby Kennedy had imposed against marching in Birmingham. So, this was King's first major rift with the Kennedy brothers. He was defying them in Birmingham, and he had gone to jail on Good Friday, April 12, a couple of weeks earlier. He had requested, as he was going into jail, that the Reverend James Bevel show up and preach for him.

Many people in this room are familiar with the Reverend James Bevel, because he worked with our organization and ran as a Vice Presidential candidate with Lyndon LaRouche in 1992. Bevel came up with a tactic, which later became known as the "Children's March." King knew nothing about it; King was in jail when Bevel came up with this. He devised this with a few of his friends, including Bernard Lafayette and one or two others. This was completely in opposition to the other members of King's staff, like Reverend Wyatt Walker and others—they were completely opposed to the tactic, because it involved taking 7-year-old and 9-year-old and 12-year-old kids, and involving them in a series of nonviolent actions. That was considered by the staff to be completely the wrong thing to do. There was a discussion about that between King and Bevel, and I won't go into that right now, because I want to make a different point, which is, that despite the fact that the Kennedy brothers opposed King, which they did, and that the March on Washington of 1963 was actually originally called by Reverend Bevel *against* the Kennedy brothers—between that point and the end of that year, there was a sudden change, and there was a congruence among the Kennedys, King, and others.

public domain

President John F. Kennedy, walking to the speaker's platform at Muscle Shoals, Alabama, May 18, 1963. Kennedy later had a "frank talk" with Governor George Wallace (arms extended).

On May 18, 1963, eight days after the Children's March had more or less concluded, with a full defeat of segregation in the city of Birmingham, President Kennedy went to Muscle Shoals, Alabama to deliver a speech, and standing next to him was George Wallace. Now, for those who aren't familiar, Mr. Wallace had become infamous for his Jan. 14, 1963 Inaugural Address as governor and for later standing in the doorway of the University of Alabama against the National Guardsmen who were there to make sure that the University was integrated. He said: "Segregation Now, Segregation Tomorrow, Segregation Forever." So, about eight days after the Children's March, President Kennedy was standing next to George Wallace in Muscle Shoals, Alabama. They were there to commemorate the 30th anniversary of the TVA. This is what JFK said on that occasion. This is not the full speech, but includes excerpts from it which are relevant. For those who come from that time, this will have a certain echo for you. Kennedy said:

> Thirty years ago today, a dream came true. President Franklin Delano Roosevelt, in the presence of TVA's two great defenders—George Norris of Nebraska, and Lister Hill of Alabama—signed his name to one of the most unique legislative accomplishments in the history of the United States. That simple ceremony, which took only a few minutes, ended a struggle which had gone on for a decade. It gave life to a measure which had been vetoed twice by two preceding Presidents—Calvin Coolidge and Herbert Hoover. In reality, this act of signature was only a beginning. There were many who still regarded the undertaking with doubts, some with scorn, some with outright hostility. Some said it couldn't be done. Some said it shouldn't be done. Some said it wouldn't be done. But today, thirty years later, it has been done.

> They predicted the government was too inefficient to help electrify the Valley, but TVA by any objective test is not only the largest, but one of the best managed power systems in the United States. They predicted, and there are always those who predict everything against something new. They predicted that a Federal, regional corporation would undermine the state governments and the local governments. But state and local governments are thriving in this Valley, and hundreds of state and local park and recreational areas have been set aside through the entire TVA. They predicted that the TVA would destroy private enterprise. But this Valley has never bloomed like it does today. Hundreds of thousands of jobs have been created because of the work that these men did before us. New forests have been built, new farms have been developed. Engineers who testified that multi-purpose

dams would not work, that rivers could not be developed for navigation, and the generation of electricity and prevention of floods at the same time, were proved wrong. Barge traffic on this system has grown from 33 million tons in 1933 to 2 billion tons today, on a river spanned by more than 30 dams. They are contributing to the life and vigor of the largest supplier of power in the United States. And as the people of this state and Valley who made this possible, I congratulate you all, because this has not been made to work in Washington. It has been made to work by the people of the Valley.

From time to time, statements are made labelling the Federal government an outsider, an intruder, an adversary. In any free federation of states, of course differences will arise, and differences will persist. But the people of this area know that the United States government is not a stranger or not an enemy. It is the people of 50 states, joining in a national effort to see progress in every state of the Union. For without the national government, without the people of the United States working as a people, there would be no TVA. Without the national government, and the people of the United States working together, there would be no protection of the family farmer, his income, and his financial independence. For he never would have been able to electrify his farm to insure his crop, to support its price, and to stay ahead of the bugs, the boll weevils, and the mortgage bankers. Without the national government and the people of the United States working together, there would be no school lunch or milk programs for our children, no assistance on conserving soil or harvesting trees, no loans to help a farmer buy his farm, and no security at the bank.

During the period of, for example, 1962 in Mississippi, you had a near civil war with the infamous General Walker, who had actually called out the Mississippi National Guard against the Federal National Guard. If you understand the process that was occurring in the United States in 1963, then you understand the significance of Kennedy's speech and what he was doing on that occasion. The idea of economic development, the idea of advanced technological progress, the idea of great projects, the idea of breakthrough technologies,

and the notion of civil rights, were arguably *one and the same idea*. But that's not what was said at the time. At the time, particularly as time went on, in 1964, 1965, 1966, and 1967, it was said that the investment in space is detracting from the civil rights movement and from the Great Society "War on Poverty" of Lyndon Johnson. The two were *opposed*, and that was the conception that was outlined. Also during that same period, as you can document looking at the history, the zero population growth disease began to spread very widely in the United States.

The Need to Actually Think

What we're going to do at this point is a slideshow I've prepared for people, so that we can abbreviate and just punctuate a few things about the space program itself. I already referenced that all the centers were in the South. We've talked a bit about the idea that these centers were premised on the Presidential conception that man would get to the Moon and would be brought back safely within the decade, as had been said by Kennedy in his famous remarks at Rice University. In that famous speech, Kennedy said:

> We choose to go to the Moon in this decade and do the other things, not because they are easy, but because they are hard, because that goal will serve to organize and measure the best of our energies and skills, because that challenge is one that we are willing to accept, one we are unwilling to postpone, and one which we intend to win, and the others, too.

The first slide [**Fig. 1**] is of the Lincoln Memorial. The reason I put this up, to start us off, is a famous quote from this man: "You can fool all of the people some of the time, and some of the people all of the time. But you can't fool all of the people all of the time."

I put that up, because that's what *was proven* last week.

That's right! And we just barely got out of it because we happened to wake up. A few of our people woke up and realized "Wait a minute! Why are we hearing this?" And then by just beginning to think about who we are, we recognized that that was actually aimed at us. Now, it wasn't aimed at us because we're a small organization. It's not that. It's because of the way in which we shaped the "double envelopment" attack on Mueller and on the coup. We shaped it with two things, as you

LPAC/Dennis Speed

remember. One was the actual exposé of Mueller; but the other, was the Land-Bridge and the United States joining the Silk Road. We've insisted that you must do these two things, and only these two things.

So, there was an assault on the people of the United States, using this character Durbin, who was lying, to change the subject—to rattle people on a matter that people have been rattled on ever since the time of Abraham Lincoln. People have been rattled on this question of not merely racism, but of slavery. Because the issue of our United States today is one of debt slavery, of intellectual slavery, and in some cases, close to real slavery also. You can't really see it in the picture—it was very late and dark—but there is an inscription which says, "I have a dream—Martin Luther King." This is at the spot where King stood in front of Lincoln, on Aug. 28, 1963. The reason I saw it, was because there were so many young people taking pictures of it. It was interesting, because at the memorial last night, the older people were all gathered around the Gettysburg Address and the Second Inaugural, and all these young people were gathered around this little piece of ground. I came over, and I realized why.

The second photo, [**Fig. 2**] I would argue, *is* the dream of Martin Luther King. It shows

a series of rockets that were used in the space program. This is Cape Canaveral, Florida.

Here I just want to repeat something which I referenced when I wrote a two-part series of articles last year: Part I; Part II. This was on the occasion of the "Hidden Figures" film. Part I was titled: "Hidden Figures: What Color is Genius?" Part II was titled: "Minds that Soar Above the Impossible." I said that "When John Glenn stepped into his Mercury capsule in February 1962, sitting atop an Atlas inter-continental ballistic missile, he undoubtedly recalled that the first test launch of an Atlas that the seven Mercury astronauts had witnessed, saw the rocket blow up in front of their eyes. Many acts of courage, however, take place not on television but outside of public view. They no less enable the leaps that society makes in conquering challenges." So, I just want to emphasize this.

I also visited the King Memorial, which is part of the Martin Luther King Center for Nonviolent Change, built by Coretta King, in Atlanta, Georgia. It exhibits a very specific statement there: "Principle #6. Nonvio-

FIGURE 2

LPAC/Dennis Speed

LPAC/Dennis Speed

lence believes that the universe is on the side of justice."

My argument in general today is going to be that this *was* the conception that King always actually represented, *sometimes against his own followers, as well as his own detractors*. That conception of nonviolence is not really different, in its moral content, than the idea of a force-free universe. This was the way in which Kepler, for example, in his conception of the orbits of the planets, thought about *the planetary harmony* as a Godly order. In one sense, you can think about his *Mysterium Cosmographicum* as a kind of theological work, as I think he thought of it.

Immortal Courage Produces Miracles

I want to say something here now about the first major loss of astronauts that happened in the American space program. [**Fig. 3**] That was Apollo 1, which was on Jan. 27, 1967. It is well known to some, but not to others. So the following is from the official NASA account:

The first Apollo command module was scheduled for launch on the 21st February of 1967. The crew of that first flight was to be Gus Grissom, Edward White, and Roger Chaffee.

On the 27th of January, 1967, the three were scheduled for some routine exercises aboard the command module as it was perched above the Saturn V-1 rocket, 220 feet above the ground.

The spacecraft, like all the previous ones, was pressurized to 16 pounds per square inch with pure oxygen. The astronauts wore suits pressurized with less pure oxygen. It was early evening, about 6:30 p.m., when a voice cried out, "Fire in the spacecraft!" Another voice cried, "Get us out of here!" Technicians on the gantry saw a sheet of flame inside the module. Wearing face masks and asbestos gloves, they tried valiantly to open the hatch, but they were driven back by the intense heat and smoke coming from the capsule. Some six minutes after that first alarm, they were able to remove the hatch. It was too late, however, for the three astronauts. They had died almost instantly in the smoke and flames that destroyed the capsule. The accident left the nation speechless with shock. These were the first astronauts to lose their lives in the line of duty.

At Canaveral, they have a special exhibit which is for Chaffee, White, and Grissom. At this point, I want to present Grissom's words from a previous press conference. Here's what he said:

If we die, we want people to accept it. We're in a risky business and we hope if anything happens to us, it will not delay the program. The conquest of space is worth the risk of life.

Because he had said that, his statement was immediately used to allow the program to go ahead. In other words, there was initially a lot of nervousness, and there was a question of whether it should be just stopped altogether. But because of his remarks, it was not stopped.

Some would like to think that the deaths of civil rights workers like Schwerner, Chaney, and Goodman[1] wouldn't be compared to this. I say: *No, you should compare them*. Because it's precisely the same thing. What was being done by the civil rights, nonviolent movement, was to suggest that the actual words of the U.S. Constitution contained real ideas that were required to be lived up to by the American people. It wasn't a question of what it literally said, it was a question of understanding the intent. In the case of the space

---

1. Murdered in Neshoba County, Mississippi in June 1964.

LPAC/Dennis Speed

program, it's a situation in which you are always exploring a new way of thinking, a new way of seeing the universe, a new way of acting on the universe. And so, I think it's valuable to reflect on the fact that this is one of the exhibits that you would see if you went down to Cape Canaveral.

The next slide is a picture of the back of the Saturn V rocket that took man to the Moon. [**Fig. 4**] There's one of those in Huntsville and there's one also in Houston.

I think we played—at one of our meetings here—the message that was read by William Anders on the occasion of the Apollo 8 orbiting of the Moon, which happened Christmas Eve 1968. It's important to set the context: Jan. 27, 1967, the accident happens, and three astronauts are killed. Apollo 8 was the first mission in which man orbited the Moon. That was the original mission that James Lovell was part of with William Anders and Frank Borman. In December 1968, these three astronauts sent a message back to Earth:

In the beginning God created the Heaven and the Earth, and the Earth was without form and void, and darkness was upon the face of the deep, and the Spirit of God moved upon the face of the waters. And God said, "Let there be light," and there was light, and God saw the light that it was good. And God divided the light from the darkness and God saw that it was good.

That was the Christmas message of the Apollo 8 astronauts, and they returned to Earth on Dec. 27.

Meanwhile, on April 4 of the same year, Martin Luther King had been assassinated, and on June 6, Robert F. Kennedy had been assassinated. So it's important to understand that the conclusion of that year saw a dramatically convulsed United States pulled together from the Moon by three astronauts, who would not have been there, except for the fact that one dead astronaut—prior to his death—had willed them and the nation to continue that mission—as had President Kennedy. As did Martin Luther King on April 3, when he said:

I've been to the mountaintop.... And I've seen the Promised Land. I may not get there with you. But I want you to know tonight, that we, as a people, will get to the promised land!
And so I'm happy, tonight.
I'm not worried about anything.
I'm not fearing any man.
Mine eyes have seen the glory of the coming of the Lord.

That conception is no different than the conception that Gus Grissom stated, when he talked about continuing with the space program.

So, as people know, we landed on the Moon with Apollo 11: Neil Armstrong, Michael Collins, and Buzz Aldrin. Michael Collins is not usually remembered (because he did not get to walk on the Moon), but he's the man who was very happy, as he said, "cause I'm getting us back!"

We all know about that success. I'm interested today in talking about the price of the successes as well as the persons that made the policies. As is known, the Apollo Project was followed by the Space Shuttle missions: Enterprise, Columbia, Challenger, Discovery, Atlantis and Endeavor. Those are the six space shuttles that we had.

LPAC/Dennis Speed

This next picture [**Fig. 5**] is Columbia, which as you know, was destroyed in an accident. This was the second accident of the space shuttle program, in 2003, in which we lost all of the astronauts as well. They were Rick Husband, who was head of the mission, Michael Anderson and Kalpana Chalwa. These are all people of different ethnicities, they were all in the space program. That was the Columbia.

Those who lost their lives in the earlier Challenger accident were Christa McAuliffe, who is the teacher that people remember, Ronald McNair, and Judith Resnik. One of the things that you see when you're at the space museum is the humanity of each individual, how different they were, their interests. And so it gives you a sense of the humanity in space.

I think this is an important thing that is understood about manned space flight: It's not that you want to have people do things that are dangerous for their own sake, but you are, in having them involved—as for example the Chinese intend to do with the mining of the Moon and as we should join them in doing: It's a way that we are all represented in the actions of the individual. In the same way that government is supposed to work! This last picture [**Fig. 6**] shows four women in space together: This is one of the little known aspects of space exploration.

In a serious sense, the concept of the International Space Station and the concept of what in the '70s—with the Russian-American missions around Soyuz and around the idea of having joint Russian-American missions in space—was a fulfillment of what Kennedy had spoken about at American University. Because he had proposed there, just so people are clear, that there should *not* be an American mission to the Moon, or a Russian mission, but a joint mission.

It's critically important that we all know or understand that there was something else that Kennedy was planning to do, something different than what actually ended up happening. Had Kennedy had his way, the worst enemy of the United States—our Cold War foe and our biggest competitor—would have joined the United States in that mission.

The Moral Basis for Political Unity

About nonviolence, Dr. King often said that *the purpose of nonviolence is to recruit the soul of the so-called oppressor*. That the nonviolence was aimed, not at public opinion, but nonviolence was aimed at recruiting the soul of the person that was committing violence against you, and that that's how you win.

Now, Malcolm X took great umbrage at this, as some of you know. Malcolm, in a famous speech, was struck by and was incredulous at a very specific phrase that Martin Luther King used to use, which was "over-

LPAC/Dennis Speed

come them with our capacity to love." Malcolm just could not process that! " 'Overcome them with our capacity to love,'—what kind of a phrase is that?!" Go listen to him, that's what he says about it.

Yet, it should be said that prior to Malcolm's death, which was on Feb. 21, 1965, he had been in Selma, Alabama. He had been in contact with the King forces for about eight months, and he had decided that he was going to work with them on voting rights. Since 1964, he had had a conception about this, called "the ballot or the bullet," about which he gave speeches. But then he went to Selma in early February 1965. He had several conversations with people, and decided that he would try to work with them. They had urged him to stay for the campaign, but he decided that he would not. And his house was firebombed, about a week after he left Selma. He was killed the week after that. But I indicate this, because this idea of collaboration of people finding their humanity, above the Earth, is a crucial idea in the concept of the entire space program.

Here's what I intend in this presentation: I hope I've been able to give you some idea of how to think, because we're going to have a discussion about that in a few minutes. Kennedy is often thought about as a kind of failed figure, or a romantic figure, or a compulsive figure. But he's not thought about in the image of Franklin Roosevelt. And the United States of 1961 is not thought about in the image of the United States of 1932-45. Yes, there are differences in the two time periods, but there's an idea that in particular, Lyndon LaRouche talked about in his book *Earth's Next Fifty Years*. And I want to get to this: This is a surprising idea that you may not have heard, or if you've read the book, you may have gone past it. And to introduce it, I want to say something here: LaRouche wrote a memorandum in 1982, which was called "The Cultural Determinants of an Anti-Missile Beam-Weapons Policy," and I'm going to quote from that first, because you'll be interested in what he had to say:

> The general technology under which a spectrum of many kinds of beam-weapons is subsumed is what appears to most at first to be a specialized aspect of physics, relativistic physics. Actually, if we trace out the history of modern science, from its roots in the grounding-work of Leonardo da Vinci nearly five centuries ago, we are obliged to recognize that all the fundamental accomplishments of modern science are rooted directly in the conceptions of relativistic physics

Library of Congress

Martin Luther King (left) talking briefly with Malcolm X in Washington, D.C. on March 26, 1964.

already understood in broad principle by da Vinci. If we study closely, as we have been elaborating this in recent times, the functional interdependency between da Vinci's discovery of hydrodynamics and his work in relativistic geometry of visible space, something very important begins to become clear to us.

I want to say something in response to this: Da Vinci was born in 1452. LaRouche has put a very important focus organizationally on the work of Filippo Brunelleschi and his completion of the Dome of the *Cathedral of Santa Maria del Fiore* in Florence in 1436, as well as on the work of Nicholas of Cusa and his writing of *On Learned Ignorance* which took place 1439-41. The discussions going on between Brunelleschi and Nicholas of Cusa on physical principles are what inform the young da Vinci, who does place his own mark on that cathedral: He was involved in the design of a perfectly spherical ball that's placed at the top of the cupola of the Brunelleschi Dome.

The important idea here that I want to indicate about what LaRouche is saying, is that if we think about these ideas not as separate branches of thought, but rather, think about them as coming out of a much more fundamental voyage of discovery of humanity, that that is what Cardinal Nicholas of Cusa was doing. Nicholas of

Cusa was not merely trying to reunify the churches: He was trying to find a common aim of mankind that all could agree to, which was transcendent of the Earth. Helga Zepp-LaRouche's work on this is groundbreaking in the same way. Let me point out that LaRouche is writing this in 1982, *prior to the adoption by Ronald Reagan of the Strategic Defense Initiative*, called a "beam weapon policy" by LaRouche.

Let's remember that the purpose of that policy, as Reagan understood, *was to end the threat of thermonuclear war*. It was actually the same thing that Kennedy was trying to do with the joint space mission to the Moon, with the Russians in 1963. Twenty years later Ronald Reagan would adopt the LaRouche beam-weapons outlook, and Lyndon LaRouche would become the most dangerous man in the world. He was seen that way and has been treated that way, since that time, by the British establishment. It was LaRouche, a World War II veteran, of course, and a proponent of Roosevelt's worldview, who with his unique breakthrough of 1952 in his work on Bernhard Riemann and relativistic physics, *and* economy, and the application of this in physical economy, who allied with former Roosevelt-supporter Ronald Reagan to actually resolve, or attempt to resolve Kennedy's intent with his space program.

Of course Kennedy wanted the United States to get to the Moon, and for the United States to be pre-eminent in space, but he did not believe that goal required conflict with another nation, just as Donald Trump does not believe that that involves conflict with Russia or with China.

This, I think, is crucial for us to understand to get a single idea about what we really mean here, by the notion of the "cultural determinants" of a policy.

Understanding Tragedy and Overcoming It

I want to, at this point, say one last thing about *Earth's Next Fifty Years*. LaRouche wrote the following:

> The communication of the meaning of any statement is to be adduced by the test of the presence of such *living words*. Only *living words* qualify as *ideas* in the strict, technical sense of the meaning of ideas. One actually knows an idea contained within a statement, by the presence or absence of that idea as an adducible *living word*, whose adduced meaning is the fruit of the same kind of mental process associated with the regenerating of an idea from indications of the specified problem it solves, as by a modern student's reliving Archytas's construction of the doubling of the cube.

And then he gives this example. He says:

> For example, the idea of knowing the circumference of the Earth becomes a *living word* in the mental processes of the user, when the user has relived the experiment through which Eratosthenes measured the great circle of the Earth, circa 200 B.C., by deep well observations from two locations in a North-South alignment within Egypt... [Alexandria and Aswan, where he measured the difference in the shadow cast by the Sun—ed.] and then measured the great-circle distance from Alexandria, Egypt to Rome by the same method.

So the idea is:

> The accumulation of such re-enactments of discoveries of proof of principle, is the required ordinary basis for the development of what we should aim to evoke as a resulting sense of scientific literacy in the adolescent mind.

What's he getting at? He actually says at one point, the way that you know an idea in a statement is—it's a discontinuity. It actually doesn't go with the rest of the statement. That's the way he puts it. So I want to give you an example of that, in the case of Lincoln. I'm going to reference the Second Inaugural Address, which Lincoln delivered in March 1865. He's trying to draw people's attention to an idea that he doesn't state. Here's what he says:

> On the occasion corresponding to this four years ago all thoughts were anxiously directed to an impending civil war. All dreaded it, all sought to avert it. While the inaugural address was being delivered from this place, devoted altogether to saving the Union without war, insurgent agents were in the city seeking to destroy it without war—seeking to dissolve the Union and divide effects by negotiation. Both parties deprecated war, but one of them would make war rather than let the nation survive, and the other would accept war rather than let it perish, and the war came.

And then he says:

One-eighth of the whole population were col-ored slaves, not distributed generally over the Union, but localized in the southern part of it. These slaves constituted a peculiar and power-ful interest. All knew that this interest was somehow the cause of the war. To strengthen, perpetuate, and extend this interest was the object for which the insurgents would rend the Union …, while the Government claimed no right to do more than to restrict the territorial enlargement of it. Neither party expected for the war the magnitude or the duration which it has already attained. Neither anticipated that the cause of the conflict might cease with or even before the conflict itself should cease. Each looked for an easier triumph, and a result less fundamental and astounding. Both read the same Bible and pray to the same God, and each invokes His aid against the other. It may seem strange that any men should dare to ask a just God's assistance in wringing their bread from the sweat of other men's faces, but let us judge not, that we be not judged. The prayers of both could not be answered. That of neither has been answered fully. The Almighty has His own pur-poses....

So what's going on here? This is the Inaugural Ad-dress of the President of the United States: there's noth-ing about budgets, there's nothing about timelines, there's nothing about taxes, there's nothing about human rights *exactly*, really, is there?

There's a discussion in which he's trying to point out to people that they believe certain things about their cause. Each side believes it, and they both say that God is on their side. But whether He's on the side of either one is still to be determined. And *this* is what he decides to present to the people of the United States, as the state of their union. It's a state of tragedy, and he continues here; I'll just go through one element, one other part here. He says:

Fondly do we hope, fervently do we pray, that this mighty scourge of war may speedily pass away. Yet, if God wills that it continue until all the wealth piled by the bondsman's two hundred and fifty years of unrequited toil shall be sunk, and until every drop of blood drawn with the lash shall be paid by another drawn with the sword, as was said three thousand years ago, so

still it must be said "the judgments of the Lord are true and righteous altogether."

So, you may not like it, but this may be what hap-pens, because that may be the way God thinks it is. And so then the conclusion of this speech:

With malice toward none, with charity for all, with firmness in the right as God gives us to see the right, let us strive on to finish the work we are in, to bind up the nation's wounds, to care for him who shall have borne the battle and for his widow and his orphan, to do all which may achieve and cherish a just and lasting peace among ourselves and with all nations.

And that is our position as of this afternoon. We're in something similar, without the physical conflict in our country, right now. Yes, the press has misrepre-sented. And yes, the press has lied. And yes, it's true that most of the people of the United States don't want to have war with one another. But it's also true that we are, this afternoon, in front of a coup, an ongoing coup; something that's been ongoing since the assassination of JFK. And it is our job to fulfill, what Lincoln and Kennedy, Roosevelt, Robert Kennedy, Martin Luther King, Malcolm X, and many others have sought to do. We do this because we are Americans. We don't do it because we are Republican or Democratic, or nonparti-san. We do it because, as patriots of a nation which un-derstands that there's a divinity in humanity, we recog-nize that the battle for the stars is a battle for ourselves.

So this is the conception that I think is actually at the root of what President Donald Trump *would* have said, and would say, concerning the space program.

Let me say one last thing about this: There will be no program unless we, the LaRouche movement, spear-head a process of creating, if you will, a new human rights movement, if you want to call it that: A move-ment on behalf of all humanity, where we take this idea of LaRouche's Four Laws and the space program as Lyndon LaRouche redefined it in conjunction with what the Chinese and the Russians are now doing, and make *that* the new movement for rights in the United States, the right to discovery, the right to become intel-ligent, the right to represent *all* of humanity, *off the planet as well as on it*. Peace is the expression, for us, of the successful creation, *utilizing the Presidency to do that*, of that condition in the United States and with hu-manity as a whole.

A SEQUEL ON ECONOMICS AS SCIENCE

The Rule of Natural Law

by Lyndon H. LaRouche, Jr.

During my most recent return flight from Europe, I employed the leisure time so afforded me, to outline a number of topics which are to be considered as more or less mandatory sequels to my Economic Science, in Short. *In this way, more on the subject of the principles of the individual's human creativity came out at the top of that list of either amplified, or added topics. When the matters before us here are reconsidered in that way, our primary subject for economics, in particular, and, science as a whole, becomes natural law, as opposed to presenting the same topics in the terms of reference of the currently popular, virtually Cartesian sort of imperialist obscenity which is usually presented in the name of "international law."*

The item which I elaborate here, is to be considered as the next in a sequence of contributions to the urgently needed account of the identity of those universal physical principles of human creativity which should now subsume virtually all competent studies of economic processes. However, it must also be said on that account, that this principled aspect of the appropriate practice of society's economic behavior, is to be considered as a subsumed feature of the true nature of mankind's existence in the universe, the nature of man's obligation to serve the mission of truly universal, "non-mathematical," natural law.

INTRODUCTION:
Substance Versus Shadow

Contrary to any remaining, wishful, contrary views on the current world situation among nations presently, the present world monetary-financial system has already entered fully into a now accelerating process of a general physical-economic breakdown-crisis. There is presently no nation which is presently exempt from the presently accelerating dive into doom. This present state of affairs would not have been inevitable, had the U.S. Government accepted those reforms which I detailed during the interval of July-September 2007. *The presently oncoming disintegration of the economies of all among the world's present nations, is to be blamed entirely on the refusal of those nations, especially the U.S.A. and its principal adversary, the British empire, to accept the reforms which I had prescribed during that July-September 2007 interval.*

What I had proposed in that July-September interval, was, essentially, a change from what had been, all along, a trend of monetarist-driven, *scientific incompetence* of the economic policies of practice, of all among those nations of this planet which had based their doctrines of practice on the intrinsically pathological, axiomatically malicious presumptions of such ideologues as John Locke, Adam Smith, Jeremy Bentham, and also apologists for their malicious lunacies, such as Karl Marx.

In This Section

It was Benjamin Franklin's mastery of the universal principles of human creativity which permitted him to play his indispensable role in establishing the American Republic. Here, a drawing of Franklin playing his invention, the glass harmonica.

prehension of those methods of immediately applied reform, without which, no remedy from an immediate, planetary plunge into general breakdown of the present economies of all nations, could be secured.

So, the underlying theme of the relevant preceding work, **Economic Science, in Short**, had been, that to understand our universe, we must reverse the customary, vicious error of classroom mathematics, to emphasize mathematics as being merely an auxiliary, subordinate doctrine, which has been superimposed formally upon physical science; we must no longer emulate the famous hoax of such as Euclid, as by adducing the notions of physical science from an essentially, merely deductive, *a-priorist* mathematics. We must view the universe as a whole, from its "top, down," from the appropriately superior role of the creative powers of the individual human mind, at that top, rather than as defined from the very foggy bottom of reductionist mathematics, such as Euclidean *a-priorism*, and statistics.

This indispensable correction must be, viewing the universe from the creative powers of the human mind, as superior to life, and life as superior to non-living processes, looking downwards, as I do here. This must now be policy, as by me, among others, through emphasizing the crucial lesson to be adduced from Academician V.I. Vernadsky's systemic distinctions of seeing the universe top-down, with the abiotic domain at the bottom, the Biosphere, higher, and both of those, in turn, as subordinated by that Noösphere which dwells, by destiny, among the stars. In doing that, I followed the precedent set by the founder of modern physical science, Cardinal Nicholas of Cusa, as in Cusa's keystone work on physical science, his **De Docta Ignorantia**. The sum-total of the work of Academician Vernadsky, when so viewed, has actually preceded in the order of the human mind, at the top, and below them, next, life, and then pre-life, always rejecting the systemic wrongness of subsuming life and humanity as subordinates-in-practice of mathematical notions of the abiotic as subsuming, first, life, and, after that, what should have been recognized as the superior power and authority of human reason expressed in the likeness of the Creator, over all of the rest.

Therefore, the indispensable intellectual remedies on which salvation of civilization immediately depends, must be premised on relevant scientific methods and conceptions which are systemically contrary to the practical implications of the presently prevalent, reductionist qualities of academic doctrines and related economics practices. It is those beliefs, which are generally accepted among governments still today, which are the infection expressed as the present, planetary, terminal pandemic of economic policies, policies which are, in themselves, the diseases from which the world's other present calamities have been derived.

Consequently, without considering precisely those issues of scientific method and principle which I have addressed in the referenced, preceding writing, and that I shall have added here, there could be no rational com-

The kernel of my approach in that work, what has become my life-long devotion, from the start of a witting commitment to this mission for my adult life, since about the time of my post-war experience in India, during 1946, to a long-needed effort, was that we must free our culture from the tyranny of both British imperialism and both *a-priorist* Euclidean geometry and kindred reductionist systems of mere mathematics, by adopting a system of thought rooted in defining those creative powers specific to mankind, powers which I came to recognize, later, as being exemplified by the discovery of the concept of universal gravitation by Johannes Kepler, a Kepler who was, on this account, the follower of that Cardinal Nicholas of Cusa who had been, in turn, the principal founder of the guiding conceptions of all competent expressions of modern science.

To this effect, I have emphasized, as I did in rejecting the lunacies of Bertrand Russell's clones Professor Norbert Wiener and John v. Neumann, that the first step toward scientific competence, is to be located in the creative powers expressed, uniquely, by the human species, as distinct from all other living species, *powers which are not expressed, essentially, in mathematical systems as such, but, rather, in those creative powers of the human mind specific to Classical artistic composition, such as Classical poetry.*

On this account, within the referenced antecedent writing, I emphasized not only that the creative powers of scientific and related discovery are situated, not within mathematics, but within the Classical artistic powers, as those of Classical poetry and music. I also emphasized, that the comprehension of this point which I have just restated here and now, depends upon the freeing of the specifically creative powers of the human mind from the habits associated with sense-certainty, by locating the actual human identity of the individual person in its expression as within the frame of Classical poetry.

As I had insisted, once more, in that location, that the fatal flaw in the prevalent view of physical science as "mathematical," or, worse, "statistical," lies in the failure of the credulous to recognize not merely the fact, but also the crucial implications of the role of the human powers of sense-perception as being merely instruments in the same sense as any laboratory instruments and their like. Instruments such as mere sense-perception, are systems which do not show us the reality of the universe which we inhabit; but, rather, show us some shadows cast by reality, rather than the actual relevant object of the experience. Our task is to decode those shadows, as the Christian Apostle Paul warned in his **I Corinthians,** 13.

True science, like Classical poetry, is defined by devotion to discovering those higher states, which are true reality.

I have therefore emphasized, as I have done again in this present report, that actual human knowledge lies in a reality which is *not seen directly* by our mental sense-apparatus, but, rather, is to be found, more directly expressed, only in that domain of the anti-reductionist, creative imagination associated with the type of Classical poetry.

Such is the nature of true law among nations, as distinct from, and opposed to those perverted notions associated with the term "the positive law," the latter a term which is a product of the heritage of the conception of imperial pagan law, such as the intrinsically imperialist depravity of Roman Law.

False Notions of Law

So, I emphasized, that under the customary procedures in negotiation among nations generally today, the true meaning of what is presently called "international law" is to be properly identified, instead, as "imperialist law," or, as that British positive law derived from the heathen Liberalism of Paolo Sarpi, a Liberalism which all true patriots of our United States have hated and defied, since the founding of what became our anti-imperialist republic. The particular such evil of Liberalism, which is often uttered in the abused name of law today, is, as under the rule of such empires of the past and present as the ancient Roman Empire, or the modern British empire of former Prime Minister Tony Blair, is a depraved notion of law, whose assumption is that of a "behaviorist's" notion of a kind of man-made universal law uttered as a replacement for, and also displacement of the natural law.

As I summarized the case in **Economic Science, in Short,** from the setting of the Peloponnesian War, through the Roman Empire and its Byzantine sequel, and through the dominant role of the Venetian domination of the international monetary systems of Europe and beyond, to the present moment, the world's political systems, excepting, chiefly, the best intervals of the history of our own United States, have been controlled by superimposed monetary systems. Only the Hamiltonian principle of sovereign national credit specification of the constitutional intention of the U.S.A.'s American System of political economy, has been a significant exception to the centrally dominant role of the imperial power of the European, traditionally Venice-centered monetary system over the world as a whole, that during all but a few exceptional intervals, as under U.S. Presidents Lincoln and Franklin Roosevelt's role during their Presidencies.

It is the extreme decadence of that London-centered monetary system which permeates and pollutes the entire world with its supremacy since the treasonous wrecking of the U.S. dollar during 1968-1973, which has made possible not only the continuing physical-economic decline of the world as a whole, since the 1973 launching of Anglo-Saudi oil-price swindle of 1973-2009, but, later, the even wilder insanity launched under the control of the U.S. economy by Britain's flunkey, Alan Greenspan, as Chairman of the Federal Reserve System.

As a result of that history, the world as a whole exists today as a victim of accumulation of a virtual world-wide hyper-inflationary monetary "bomb" building up under what is currently the greatest rate of deflationary collapse of real production and income of every nation of the world as a whole. The present world monetary-financial system is now going out of existence, soon, while the physical economies of nations are at the brink of a general, complete physical breakdown-crisis of the planet in its entirety.

The only remedy available for all, or any national economy of the entire world today, is the cancellation of the present world monetary systems through an ordered action of bankruptcy of all monetary systems, through a prompt, concurrent reorganization in bankruptcy, through the entire replacement of all monetary systems by the cooperative installation of a system of cooperating nation-states in launching a fixed-exchange-rate system based on a treaty organization assembled from among perfectly sovereign national credit-systems of the type inherent in the U.S. Federal Constitution.

The lawful mechanism for bringing this rescue-action about is the same principle of natural law adopted by the U.S. Federal Constitution. The authority for determining credit, prices, and guaranteed national credit for physical-economic development must come from relevant principles of natural law. The implementation of such a rescue of the nations, must be crafted on the foundation of the notion of a physical economy, rather than a monetary system. This must be based on a notion of natural law which expels monetarism.

This requires some discussion.

Otherwise, without that reform, the present situation of the nations of the world is a hopeless one, for generations still to come.

All hangs, therefore, on an adequate grasp of that meaning of "natural law" which I supply here.

Leibniz's Natural Law

What saved me from the mistakes of my more important rivals among economists, has been, first of all, the influence of Gottfried Leibniz on me from about the age of 14-15, and, later, since my embrace of it by January-February 1953, principally, Bernhard Riemann's work, his 1854 habilitation dissertation, most emphatically.

Principles of natural law also apply to situations defined by one or another form of combat, as in this case of combat between the present world monetary system, which menaces all mankind, and the opposing force of an economy based on a physical principle of natural law.

The proper standard of law for the use of the term "natural law," is that it meets the requirement of being a body of "discovered," rather than "positive" law, as, similarly, in an anti-empiricist mode in physical science, as typified by Johannes Kepler's uniquely original discovery of the principle of Solar gravitation. As, similarly, in the case of the uniquely original discovery of the principle of universal gravitation by Kepler, the discovery of the generation of a previously existing natural law, which is also a natural law which is contrary to the opinions of all silly academic dupes who believe in the mere myth of an alleged discovery of gravitation by the silly Sir Isaac Newton.

What has been merely alleged to have been Newton's formula, which was essentially a plagiarist's copy of the mathematical expression of characteristics already as defined, uniquely, by Johannes Kepler, was adopted by "the Brutish" ideologues, as a convenient image of the effect of gravitation, an image which they copied from Kepler's original work, while saying nothing of the way in which the discovery of the effect known as that form of image had been defined by Kepler. True physical laws are not mechanical-mathematical contraptions added to a Cartesian repertoire, such as those of the same foolish, Cartesian fantasy permeating British empiricist doctrines respecting science still today. As Albert Einstein emphasized, gravitation as it was defined uniquely by Kepler, reflects a power which contains the physical universe as a conceptually finite oneness, a universe as if contained by a principle of universal gravitation. That formulation for expressed gravitation, is a reflection of the finiteness of the universe, as Einstein recognized this implication of what had been, uniquely, Kepler's discovery.

President Barack Obama, for example, is not a morally decent sort of lawyer, a fact which his practice, since his entering the office of the U.S. President, has fully demonstrated to have been a grievous fault in either his nature, his development, or both. His is a radically egotistical, false law of the narcissist, one of the type of the reckless, feckless, and immoral gambler, the pirate's law called "winner take all." Only his utter defeat in his reckless, immoral enterprises could bring that fault under some significant degree of civilized control.

In fact, in his special case as representative of such a type, his moral and intellectual disabilities have been shown to be, essentially, those of a man suffering from what is to be classed, specifically, as of the variety of narcissist classed as the victim of "a Nero Complex."[1] This nature of his personal disability, has been shown most prominently since his own, and his wife's visit to meet with the Queen of England and with the Queen's husband, Prince Philip, who is a leading proponent of the pro-genocidal cult of flagrantly anti-science lies known as the World Wildlife Fund. I refer to a fault conceived in Obama's caricature of himself, which is not only akin to that of the Nazi dictatorship in Germany, but, as Obama's proposed "health reform" shows, is a product, and faithful copy of the same British cult from which the infamous pro-genocide, 1939-1945 practice of the Hitler regime was originally derived, then, as now.

There can be no competent doubt of the President's personal moral and intellectual incompetence for the office to which he has been elected, once we have taken into account his adoption of the Hitler-echoing doctrines of his retinue of so-called "Behaviorist economists," as expressed by his reliance upon his retinue of the morally and intellectually depraved, such as Larry Summers and Peter Orszag.

From a Judeo-Christian View

What I have just written here in these foregoing, opening paragraphs of this report, thus far, is said from the standpoint of a truly natural law, as the essence of the Mosaic tradition and Christianity typify that which converges, in practice, upon an expression of what we must regard as an expression of natural law, in effect: I refer, thus, to the natural relationship of the needs of the human immortal personality to the requirements of the Creator of the Universe, as the first chapter of **Genesis** typifies this, as being the natural moral requirements for a proper human existence.

In contrast to the moral and intellectual failures of President Obama, the discovery of universal physical

Johannes Kepler met the standard of natural law by "discovering" the principle of Solar gravitation, with the aid of his concept of the universe in terms of Plato's regular solids. His heuristic model of the inscribed solids is shown here.

____

1. LaRouche LPAC webcast, April 11, 2009.

principles, such as Johannes Kepler's uniquely original, and uniquely valid principle of gravitation, typifies those matters which fall under the categorical conception of *a body of natural law*. However, this is the case today precisely as an outcome of the fact, that Kepler's discovery was rooted in the work of the great modern scientist and theologian Nicholas of Cusa's definitions of those principles of natural law from which Kepler derived his subsumed, uniquely original and valid discovery of gravitation.

Natural law, so defined, is the only principle of law rightfully imposed upon a nation and its elaboration of a morally tolerable form of positive law; all decent law is, thus, premised on this conception of all mankind, as a species, as made in the principled likeness of the Creator. This same notion was delivered to the formation of our own republic, through Gottfried Leibniz's influence, in his condemnation of the evil of John Locke's active promotion of Africans' slavery. Leibniz emphasized the necessary shaping of what we adopted as our constitutional law of the Declaration of Independence and the Preamble of our U.S. Federal Constitution. That Constitution has served, from its launching, as the model of the international law which was adopted as the basis for the existence of our Federal Republic, and the foundation of any international law tolerable to our republic.

For example, our U.S. Constitutional law was derived chiefly, and most directly, from the influence of Leibniz's contributions to universal science, in opposition to the intrinsic depravity of the notions of law associated with the British Empire's adoption of the evil, Ockhamite tradition of Paolo Sarpi, and, from what was so derived from that same root of medieval Ockhamite irrationalism, such as the pro-slavery dogma of John Locke, or the utter depravity of Adam Smith and Jeremy Bentham.

Such is the view from the standpoint of our own republic's notion of the natural law, a natural law which coincides with the affirmations presented in the great U.S. Constitutional principle, of human happiness, that of Leibniz, which we meet at the center of our Declaration of Independence and the Preamble of our Federal Constitution. It is a notion which has been in deadly opposition to that opposing, imperial tradition of law, against which our patriots fought, against the evil oppression and perversion of law which has been the law and contemporary offshoots of the merely positive law of the British Empire, such as that of Adam Smith's obscene **Theory of Moral Sentiments**, and in the center

of our republic's rejection of those obscene adversaries of the true natural law.

So, if we continue the argument for discovered natural law, rather than what is known and concocted as the merely concocted choice of positive law, we come to the aspect of natural law which sets the human individual apart from the beasts, as from the British imperialists, and their Roman imperialist predecessors, alike. The proper ruling law of the U.S.A., for example, is the natural law as expressed by our 1776 Declaration of Independence, and, as the Preamble of our Federal Constitution expresses influences consistent with that relevant opinion of Gottfried Leibniz which is embodied in our U.S. Declaration of Independence.

This, our republic's founding principle, was derived from the notion of natural law for mankind in the universe, and was adduced as consistent with Leibniz's specified distinction of a body of law which opposed contrary conceptions, especially those implicitly imperialist conceptions of a merely positive law which were demanded by such pro-Satanic spokesmen for the British Empire today, as former British (or, perhaps, better said, "brutish") Prime Minister Tony Blair. Contrary to the evil sophist Blair and his like, our republic's constitutional law is not a positivist's law, but *a body of discovered universal law*, as in the same sense of that as is given to us by the example of the discovered universal physical principles of science.

The Matter of Physical Science

Keep that image in mind. The future of the universe, and of mankind within it, is brought forth, in each forward step, by a higher authority than anything previously presumed to be known. In this matter, it is not such law which has been limited, thus far; it is mankind's knowledge of that open body of law which is limited. This discovery of an already needed, newly discovered principle of the universe, and of human behavior within it, always comes from outside of that which had been viewed, mistakenly, earlier, as being already completely predetermined. That is the proper general definition of human creativity, which proceeds not to completeness, but to the discovery of the perpetual incompleteness of our progress in dealing with both our experience and knowledge to date, and also with the revolutionary evolution of the universe itself to higher states of being.

That distinction is the approach which will bring us to that higher standpoint in science, where we gain the

Albert Einstein, shown here playing the violin in the New Synagogue of Berlin in January 1930, represented the higher standpoint in science, as expressed by Leibniz's concept of dynamics.

knowledge required to assure our continued efforts on behalf of the existence of mankind. That is the outlook which I present in these pages. The proof of the point is to be made relatively clearer, as follows.

By "higher standpoint," or, in the alternative expression, "underlying," I am pointing, as I shall explain, again, here, at a later point, to an open-ended approach to higher expressions of that concept of *dynamics,* as *dynamics* was defined for modern science by Gottfried Leibniz, or by the haunting, "tensor-like" conception represented by the concluding paragraph of Percy Bysshe Shelley's **A Defence of Poetry**.[2]

As I had emphasized in my just published **Economic Science, in Short,** Academician Vladimir Ivanovich Vernadsky, of Russia and Ukraine, has supplied those relevant discoveries of his conceptions of the natural partition of physical space-time among the phase-spaces of the *abiotic, Biosphere,* and *Noösphere.* In his bringing modern science, thus, to a higher standard for

the sense of a universal body of natural law, he went outside, beyond, and above what had been mistaken for completed knowledge earlier. These three universal phase-spaces represent a certain set of which all are of crucial relevance at this time of the present world crisis. It is the Noösphere which expresses that principle of universality by which the universe is directed, top down. It is in such progress into matters not known to practice earlier than that, through which mankind rises out and away from impending doom, to the relative security of a higher state of human existence than had existed before.

That might be restated as follows.

Genesis!

The connection which was often missed in the effort to adduce the practical implications of the singularly awesome, opening chapter of **Genesis**,[3] has been missed as the result of a lack of an adequate comprehension of that specific significance of the same notion of *creativity per se* which I have presented as the keystone feature of that leading work just published earlier on this same subject: the subject of *the specific uniqueness* of *human creativity* as contrasted with the essential quality of any other known form of inanimate or living existence.[4]

Therefore, here, I emphasize the continuing significance, for this present and subsequent publications, of my decision to include the appended "In Short" in the title of the preceding published work. My intent here is to emphasize that that piece, when considered as a whole, provided a truthful account, but only as in a summary of what is still required for a continuing series of extended treatments of those topics which I identified there, as I do, again, now.

The further elaboration of one, crucially important

---

2. Essentially, Leibniz's *dynamics* (**Specimen Dynamicum**, 1695) echoes the *dynamis* of the Pythagoreans and Plato, and also anticipates the conception of the physical principle of the tensor, as by the leading work of Bernard Riemann, Albert Einstein, and Academician V.I. Vernadsky. For the significance of dynamics in social processes, as for Shelley, see relevant references below.

3. I do not include the "Adam and Eve story" in this characterization; rather, I attribute that to a hostile, Mesopotamian genesis. It is also notable, that the actual universe is neither "completed" in any way, nor can it be completed. The actual universe is anti-entropic, and, as Albert Einstein emphasized, never completed, or completable in any prevalent sense of the term "completed," today. The notion of "completed" is an expression of an *a-priorism* which is merely typified by the fraudulent assumptions of Euclid, as also similar varieties of reductionist a-priorism.

4. As I have emphasized elsewhere, creativity does exist within the Biosphere, as this is expressed by the emergence of successively higher orders of living plant and animal. Creativity expressed by the human will, which is my point here, occurs among no known living species other than mankind.

example of that notion, is required for treating a particular aspect of the subject of creativity, an aspect now treated more fulsomely in this present location. This present writing here, also precedes anticipated, subsequent publications which, when written, will have presented a series of comparable treatments of some highly relevant, other leading topics identified, in a preliminary way, in that completed set of relevant earlier pieces.

The mission so defined, is the role of mankind in the specific labor of developing the universe itself to higher states, that according to the mission for man and woman implicitly specified in the opening chapter of **Genesis**.

During the brief time in which the already completed, introductory report of this series has been in circulation, the "In Short" part of the title of that report, has already attracted what I had intended to provoke as a certain, fruitful kind of anxiety about certain matters. As I have just indicated here above, that work was composed to provoke as much anxiety about more or less popular, false assumptions, as it did answers. It was essential to the intended end-result, to promote and sustain, a state of internal intellectual tension which should serve as an introduction to the following, present, in-depth treatment of my launching of what is a matter of presently great importance for the benefit of mankind as a whole, and in the matter of a science of physical economy, in particular.

So, this current work in progress, when considered as a whole, was intended, in effect, to lead to a needed, more fulsome presentation of each of the collateral topics which I have invoked, in presenting the urgent need for presenting a science of physical economy, not merely as a long overdue change in outlook, but what must now replace what has now become, almost entirely, the disastrously failed, present methods otherwise extant in the professionals' practice of political-economy, in the policies of all nations, everywhere, today.

The Trouble with Popular Opinions

The follies permeating the current, egomaniacal policy-shaping of a Nero-like President Barack Obama, and the already ruinously foolish performance met in all the work of his predecessor, are key elements of the presently extreme case of a trend in economic and social policy-shaping which has become an absolute disaster, for other nations as also our own—indeed, for our planet as a whole. This has been the ugly trend toward a new rise of fascism in the Americas and Europe, today, even globally, since, in fact, about the time of the March 1, 1968 turn in economic affairs, which accompanied the emergence of the full-blown, venereal, Dionysian rage of fascism which was only typified by the 1968-69 role of Mark Rudd at Columbia University and related environs, increasingly, during the remainder of that and the following years, up to the present day.

It is important to emphasize, that I have been provoked to this present step of a radical revision of all existing national economic systems, out of my decades-long progress as being what is, in fact, presently, a leading known economist: probably, by standards of performance in forecasting, the leading economist in the world today. My emerging role to this present effect, came through a variety of converging current circumstances, including the issues posed among serious, presently working economists, and others similarly occupied, for the presentation of a new, general conception of the principles of a science of physical economy. Those sequels, such as this in progress here, must be called into general use, if a successful, much-needed, and very radical change in the practice of "economics" is to become available now.

Although the already published portion of my still ongoing recent work to this effect, has included a certain amount of reference to the roots and role of creativity in any possible form of human society, what I had provided up to this moment, while accurate as far as it goes, has been only preliminary with respect to what remains to be done, stepwise, in the relatively immediate future. At this same time, the world is confronted with the urgent need for doing a bit more than to simply put a presently bankrupt world into some urgently needed form of reorganization, as I had proposed just such a relatively immediate remedy, for my own part, quite successfully, during July-September 2007. The wildly insane measures taken, by the U.S. government, and also relevant other leading national powers, since September 2007, have created what has now become a global disaster for all humanity, a development which has now gone beyond any tolerable limit for every part of humanity as a whole. The time for mere reform has passed; the time for a revolution in the notion of economy, has arrived. On this account, what is urgently needed, as I have already emphasized here, is something which is not merely a reform, but an entirely new way of thinking about economy. That is my duty and intention, as expressed again here.

The outbreak of Dionysian rage in 1968-69, as epitomized by provocateur Mark Rudd at Columbia University (shown here), represented a turning point toward fascism, and an abandonment of a commitment to principled science.

The mission here may be summed up fairly, as follows.

The Franklin Roosevelt Legacy

The presently onrushing, monstrous failure of the world's economy in general, throughout the sweep of the time since what has been shown to have been the calamitously premature death of U.S. President Franklin Roosevelt, and up to the time of the presently onrushing, global breakdown-crisis of the world at large, compels us to adopt what are, for nearly everyone today, fundamentally new conceptions respecting economy in general. There are new conceptions respecting new kinds of relations among national economies, novelties which must now be overthrown entirely, many among which have been long considered as axiomatic truths, but are, as they have been now shown to have been, the presently, brutally failed principles which had come, unfortunately, to be generally accepted among nations.

The notion of formal, deductive systems, as often supplied as a substitute for creative science, confines the mind to that deductionist's prison, called sense-certainty, such as that of the founders of a modern reductionist, positivist, or even worse mathematics which have been adopted, in practice, as a replacement for actual science. They are typified, still today, by the earlier attacks on Leibniz by such perverts as the followers of Abbe Antonio Conti and Voltaire, such as Abraham de Moivre, D'Alembert, the scoundrel and turncoat Leonhard Euler, Adrien-Marie Legendre, Pierre-Simon Laplace, Augustin Cauchy, or Rudolf Clausius and Herrmann Grassmann, and London-linked Hermann von Helmholtz.

The essence of competence in science, mathematical or otherwise, is to recognize the smell of intellectual death in such as the work of Aristotle, Aristotle's scoundrelly heir Euclid, or all others who rely upon an a-priorist, deductive model in place of, and in opposition to that process of overthrowing of all deductive systems, a process upon which competent Classical poetry and science depend absolutely.

The notion of a purely mathematical physics, as by the adversaries of Leibniz, Einstein, and others, hangs upon the legacy of the *a-priorist* followers of Aristotle, such as Euclid.[5] From this legacy, and expressed by the even more radical corruption of the Ockhamite followers of Paolo Sarpi, comes the modern European mental illness known as an essentially deductive mathematics with its notion of the proximate "completeness" of a sufficiently extended array of present, formal mathematical systems.

Therefore, the satanic Olympian Zeus, and all his Delphic-like doctrines, be damned; I begin with the most essential of those topics which were identified in the previous paper's summary of the nature and role of the creative powers of the human mind in defining a physical economy.

The significance of what I have condemned as that widespread popularity of the notion of the science achievable through a search for consistency of mathematics through deductive extension, is the pathology of which science, together with the **New York Times** style book, must cleansed, in order that honest creativity might be freed from the inherent, corrupting stagnation of the contemporary formalists.

---

5. This is not to speak of the more obscene systems of belief and practice familiar to the earlier Middle East.

I. An Essential Recapitulation

To get down directly to the chief business at hand, when we view the present world-wide situation rightly, we appear to be, already, throughout this planet, at least arguably so, now almost as much as doomed and dead; that becomes a certainty, if presently prevalent trends in opinion about science, such as the obscene, virtually Satanic, genocidal lie of "global warming," are permitted to be continued. This is not for reason of the currently surging global pandemic, a pandemic which may, or may not be chiefly from "natural causes." The character of the problem is, that it reflects the deteriorated, general physical conditions of life which recently, or, currently prevalent politics, have brought down upon the planet as a whole, especially since the global, existentialist, moral catastrophe of Spring 1968.

The foul corruption responsible for this condition, has been fostered under the present global circumstances of a general monetary and physical-economic breakdown-crisis, a crisis radiating from the global system of monetarist powers centered in the evil radiating from the virtual empire of the monetarist United Kingdom: that United Kingdom which has been operating according to the so-called "green" policies of the pro-genocidal, essentially pro-satanic World Wildlife Fund of Prince Philip et al., and according to the continuing complicity in this evil, by the current President of the United States, especially so since the 1968-1973 interval, to the present date.

In the earlier, substantial, introductory portion of this presently continuing series, I centered the reader's attention on the distinction between two available, voluntary types of choices of an operating sense of personal identity in society today. The first choice, what I have identified as a defective state of mind, has, unfor-

Lord Bertrand Russell took a leading role in establishing the satanic genocidal policies of the British empire, which threaten civilization today.

UNESCO/C. Bablin

tunately, usually been the location of the individual's optional sense of personal identity, as expressed, typically, in terms of the crude belief in sense-certainty. It is that influence which has continued to be the customary location of that which the usual individual regards, what is for him, as his, or her intra-social expression of personal identity. In my own, contrary, preferred choice, I locate the individual's properly chosen sense of his, or her personal identity, quite differently. It is notable that I do so out of my included great respect, even sometimes awe, for what the greatest scientific minds and Classical artistic geniuses have accomplished on relevant accounts.

That much said thus far, to open the following chapter, I shall continue my account by noting, that in the modern physical science which flowed from the work of such geniuses as Brunelleschi, Nicholas of Cusa, Leonardo da Vinci, Johannes Kepler, Pierre de Fermat, and Gottfried Leibniz, the distinction of the creative personality, lies presently in the recognition of *the ontological actuality* of the so-called "infinitesimal" of the Leibniz calculus, as opposed to such follies as the corrupted version of the calculus associated with such perverts as the hoaxster (and sometime plagiarist) Augustin Cauchy.

A Role for the Tensor

While the distinction which I have just emphasized in the immediately preceding paragraphs, is already formally correct, there is a still deeper—much deeper—issue of scientific method involved. It goes as follows.

The organization of evidence for purposes of a process of physical-scientific discovery of principle, begins, as it must, with reference to the role of experimental experience in the employment of powers of sense-perception. This includes not only what may be recognized as the individual person's "native senses," those which are delivered somewhere along the course leading to the birth of the new individual, but also includes artificial senses comparable to the category of scientific instruments, such as telescopes and microscopes, or sundry varieties of heat-sensing devices employed in exploring behavior in the extremely large, or in the extremely small.[6]

However, while the experience of sense-perception is essential for the development of knowable, effective human power for inducing change in the universe, the paradoxical relationship among differing specific modes of experience presents us with many mutually contradictory presumptions, such as those of the fabled blind men and the elephant, as to what the real universe is, actually. We are brought, thus, to the point, that the paradoxes of sense-experience associated with different choices of natural, or synthetic sensory experiences, confront us with the practical need for what have come to be known as universal physical principles: *principles which are not defined by sense-perceptual experience as such, but, rather, by the fact of what are the mutually contradictory results among the categories of sensory experience. This includes not only the experience of the given, inborn, biological senses, but also the artificial ones, such as those of scientific instrumentation.*

Modern Science as Such

On account of the fruits of those combined sources of evidence, in all modern physical science, the discovery, uniquely, by the follower of Nicholas of Cusa's founding of modern science,[7] Johannes Kepler, of the principle of universal gravitation within the Solar system considered in the large, has become, as Albert Einstein emphasized, the unique foundation of universal systemic scientific competence within the domain of applied modern physical science.

Therefore, for reason of our reliance upon that ironically juxtaposed experimental evidence on which competent scientific practice depends, we must emphasize the role of the *tensor*, in addressing all matters bearing on any contemporary proof of universal prin-

ciple. We must define the role of the tensor in such terms, but not the often deceptive standpoint of the mathematician as such, the reductionists excluded most emphatically.

Those distinctions just summarized, are to be considered as follows.

What we recognize, through our powers of sense-perception, is not the real universe we inhabit, but only a kind of shadow cast by that universe's existence, shadows such as those cast as sense-perceptions, or by instruments such as those which are employed to extend the reach of the mind to the very large or very small.

An Anti-Entropic Universe

The common root of the systemic moral failures in most of taught scientific education and related subject-matters, is what is typified by what Philo of Alexandria exposed as the Aristotelean perversion of the teaching of geometry, a teaching which remains, still today, the hereditary principle of intellectual rotting traced, variously, to Euclidean geometry, and to related forms of intellectual perversion, such as modern empiricism. These are exemplary of the cases which implicitly presume a methodologically deductive array of scientific and comparable knowledge, a prevalent academic and related perversion which has been premised on a system of deductively polluted consistency, called, with farcical solemnity, mathematics, which undercuts and ruins the creative potential of the minds of most trained professionals and related cases, still today.

We live in a self-developing, anti-entropic universe, not one of a fixed, deductive design. Hence, the influence of the mystical dogma of "universal entropy" on the minds of so many among our academic specialists in mathematics, makes them become more or less rabidly insane by about the time they come to enjoy what is termed, quite ironically, a "terminal degree."

For example, Kepler came to recognize, as in his **The Harmonies of the Worlds**, that neither the application of the sense of a visible line of sight, nor of musical harmonics, could define the principle of organization of the Solar system as known to Europe up to that time. However, a paradoxical juxtaposition of the two alternately presumed notions of a general ordering factor, sight and harmonics, provided the remedy, and yielded the same general law of gravitation plagiarized from Kepler's own original discovery by the custodians

---

6. As Bernhard Riemann emphasized in his 1854 habilitation dissertation, it is the ironical changes from all customary notions of sense-perception, as these are encountered in the very large or very small, which present us with the relatively most crucial ideas respecting the general laws of the universe.

7. **De Docta Ignorantia** (1440 A.D.).

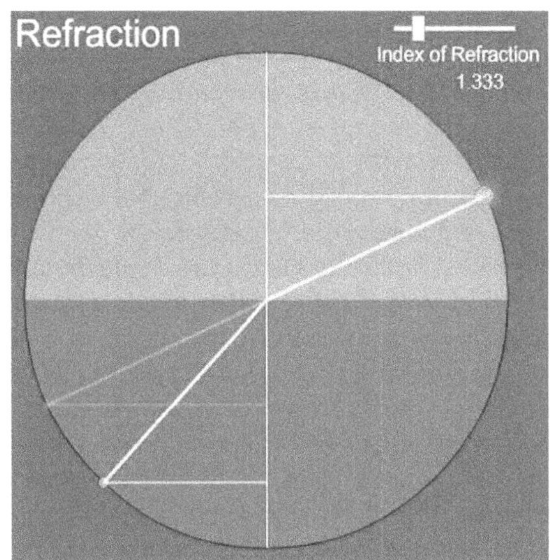

Among the leading experiments which blasted apart the Euclidean concept of time and space was that of Pierre de Fermat (right), showing how light changed course from a straight line when passed through different media. A schematic is shown here.

of a curiously mad and scientifically inept black-magic specialist Isaac Newton.

In a similar fashion, Sky Shields' recently published mapping of the actual process of discovery represented by Carl F. Gauss' discovery of the orbit of Ceres, unveils the actual workings of the creative mind of Gauss in his original discovery of the asteroid orbits.

All true universal physical principles, as known, show that same type of ironical composition. Hence, the singular importance of the work of Bernard Riemann's discoveries in bringing the use of tensor-like methods of Gauss to its proper place in the general repertoire of physical scientific methods. Sky Shields' application of the tensor to craft a physical, rather than simple image of the orbit of Ceres, illustrates a point which is applicable to all cases of discoveries of a generally true physical principle in any domain, *including a competent science of physical economy.*

Euclid's Relevant Great Crime

There are three methods available in modern scientific practice, for defining a general principle. The typical model in European civilization today, although incompetent, is that associated with the model of Euclidean geometry. The assumption is, "Is the assumed principle true in all possible cases?" While that guideline may appear suited to abstract Euclidean or an "imperfectly Euclidean" variety of formal geometry, as

by Lobatchevsky, it fails to meet the standard which must be required of a presented case of physical science. This distinction was made clear with the appearance of Bernhard Riemann's 1854 habilitation dissertation, in which no *a-priorist* assumptions were permitted in the domain of physical geometry. Since Riemann's habilitation dissertation, all later competencies in physical geometry were defined by relevant conceptual methods of physical experiment, rather than implicitly *a-priorist* formal geometries.[8]

At least, that was true in principle; in practice, the matter was not so simple.

The universe of Bernhard Riemann, and of such followers of Riemann as Albert Einstein and V.I. Vernadsky, is a kind of physical universe in which the most underlying characteristic of action is the emergence of new, more truthful kinds of physical dimensionality. Today, since the work of Vernadsky, in ordering physical-scientific practice, we should examine such qualitative changes associated with a self-evolving physical geometry, evolving with those kinds of qualitative changes in the periodic table of physical biochemistry which we associate with evolutionary changes in quality among the abiotic, living, and human-cognitive

---

8. It is important to reference the correspondence of Carl F. Gauss with such as Farkas and Janos Bolyai, and with others, on the ruckus stirred up by Gauss' warnings to Jonas Bolyai on the subject of Jonas' claim to have discovered a principle of non-Euclidean geometry. The same criticism is extended to the claims for a Lobatchevskian geometry. The implied method expressed by Gauss's discovery of the Ceres orbit indicates the truth of the matter. The Nineteenth-century history of the subject of a "non-Euclidean" geometry was posed by the most famous of the teachers of Gauss, Abraham Kästner. Gauss, in his letters to the Jonas and Farkas Bolyai, and to others, on this matter, emphasizes that he had discovered a non-Euclidean geometry (premised on provocations in the work of his teacher, Kästner) during his studies of the middle through late 1790s. The application of the relevant tensor approach to Gauss's solution for the orbit of Ceres, shows that Gauss was actually using such a anti-Euclidean geometry in that discovery.

qualities of physical phase-spaces of the universe considered as an integrated whole.

Today, with the appearance of any newly considered universal physical principle, no previously existing geometry can satisfy the notion of completeness within the bounds of any formal geometry. There is no longer any competent equivalent of such presumed systems extended to completion "in infinity" as a Euclidean geometry.

There are two most notable transformations to consider on this account.

First, we must take into account, that sense-perceptions present us with no better than the kinds of shadows cast by the real universe, rather than the real universe as such. Second, since the work of Academician V.I. Vernadsky, we are properly obliged to view the universe of our experience as one in which the Noösphere *as defined, functionally*, subsumes the Biosphere, and the Biosphere, in turn, subsumes the abiotic domain. The definition used for this purpose is supplied by the question: which domain changes which?

Nonetheless, in the struggle of scientists to make a career, so to speak, they were often obliged, to suppress their fidelity to strictly scientific principles, out of a generally imposed requirement to show a certain degree of consideration for *a-prioristic* geometries modeled, more or less, on the widely approved fantasy known as Euclidean geometry. So, to survive in the practice of their professional career in science, they found it expedient to, at least, pretend that they believed in the test of deductive completeness as an idealized, entropic standard, imposed arbitrarily, for any generally accepted practice of geometry. Curiously, and, also, not so curiously, the product of exploring the domain of physical geometry from the standpoint of the assumed principle of axiomatic completeness for any geometry, turned out to have its heuristic merits within the domain of the ante-room to a physical-scientific form of geometry, as this is illustrated by the explorations conducted under the direction of the famous David Hilbert.

However, thanks given to Hilbert for exposing the assumption he tested, the universe is actually anti-Euclidean, as Hilbert helped to demonstrate this after his fashion.

Since I am writing this work, some account for my own history in respect to these matters has a certain, much more than passing relevance for the purposes of my account here.

II. My View of This Matter

In entering this chapter of the report, we must recognize two crucial features of my point, First, that I am not only an economist of notable, largely unique achievements in long-range forecasting, but that the highest form of known physical existence in our universe is the role of discoveries of the universal physical principles which underlie the notion of a physically successful economy as a whole.

The related problem has been, not that our scientists have been stupid; rather, they have been forbidden to bring the crucial physical evidence of universal and related economic principles into the domain of my particular expertise, the science of physical economy.

Since all matters of physical chemistry's role in economies lie within my domain of principal practice, the chief source of the failures of policy-shaping among modern nation-states has been that the most crucially important aspect of physical science, the economic progress of mankind, has been abandoned to the Delphic frauds of a pro-Satanic class of political-economic religious ideologues, such as our leading financial accountants and bureaucrats of kindred superstitions.

The essential failure common to both most practice of economics and financial accounting, is typified by the fraudulent approach of Laplace colleague Augustin Cauchy to the subject of the calculus. Following the school of Eighteenth-century Leibniz-haters such as Abbe Antonio Conti, Voltaire, Jean le Rond D'Alembert, Leonhard Euler, and Laplace, the factor of change which defines a science of reality, the Leibniz infinitesimal, was suppressed by the systemically reductionist pagan priesthoods of mathematics.

What is fairly described as the uniqueness of my own successes as an economic forecaster, beginning the middle of the 1950s, was rooted, on the one side, in my recognition, since early adolescence, of the intrinsic absurdity of any formal geometry similar to that of Euclidean geometry. This defined the basis for my subsequent adoption of the standpoint of Gottfried Leibniz's condemnation of the inherently systemic fraud of the work of Descartes, in favor of Leibniz's adopted standpoint of that principle of *dynamics*, which has underlain all higher development in the progress of physical science, as to matters of principle, since that time. The collaboration of Leibniz with Jean Bernouilli, in applying consideration of Pierre de Fermat's principle of least

Lyndon LaRouche's outstanding achievements in rely heavily on his rejection of formal Euclidean geometry, and commitment to discovering dynamic physical principles. Here, he is examining a machine at the Escorts Tractor Plant in India, during a 1982 visit.

science was that, if, sense-perceptions are merely shadows cast upon the mind, rather than the actual objects which have cast those shadows: *what, then, is the knowable expression of the differences between reality, on the one side, and the shadows cast on human opinion by the experience of that wrongly conceived reality known as "sense certainty," on the other.* The implication of this, in turn, forces us to consider the implication of the evidence, as Leibniz adduced his discovery and subsequent development of the concept of the differential calculus from the implications of the successive work of such as Kepler and Pierre de Fermat. *The reality of experience lies not in the perceived object, or its idealization as such, but in those kinds of actual, efficient changes in perceived state, which violate, experimentally, the notion of deductions from merely apparent sense-certainty?* Leibniz's definition of *dynamics*, as a revived expression of the principle of *dynamis* expressed by Classical *Sphaerics*, as in the duplication of the cube by Archytas, and the consequences of this for Archytas' associate Plato, defined the universal physical principle specific to both Leibniz's original definition of the calculus, in 1675, the addition of *dynamics*, during the 1690s, and his enhanced reworking of this as a universal, catenary-tractrix-cued, physical principle of least action, as cast in collaboration with Jean Bernouilli.[9]

In other words, between the view of real experience implied by notions of sense-certainty, and the real universe, there is a gap expressed, typically, by that notion of the "infinitesimal" whose existence Euler, with bare-

action to elaborate a general principle of universal physical least action, has been considered by me as the continuing mainstream of inspiration for all truly principled accomplishments, such as those of Carl F. Gauss and Bernhard Riemann, since.

This led me, in turn, to come to the view that sense-perceptions were not realities, but shadows of reality. In this way, I came to the related view, that the definition of the infinitesimal by Leibniz expressed the essential difference between the real universe we experience, his view, and the shadow-like images of that experience associated with naive sense-certainty, his adversaries' view.

The attacks on Leibniz's work by empiricist followers of the Ockhamite irrationalism of Paolo Sarpi, were to be traced, during the Eighteenth Century, through such accomplices of the hoaxster Rene Descartes, as the set of empiricists led by Abbe Antonio Conti and Voltaire, to hoaxes such as those which are to be traced to the hoaxsters Abraham de Moivre and D'Alembert, who concocted the hoax of "imaginary numbers," and, later, the less exotic trick of simply denying the existence of the Leibniz "infinitesimal" by the opportunist hoaxster Leonhard Euler (who knew better than to actually believe his own rubbish on this account).

The issue so posed to Eighteenth-century physical

---

9. The notion of a physical geometry which underlies Leibniz's notion of dynamics, is traced in modern European science to the role of the catenary (the "funicular" form of physical curve) employed by Filippo Brunelleschi for the construction of the cupola of Florence's **Santa Maria del Fiore,** and the development of the pairing of the catenary and tractrix relationship by Leonardo da Vinci.

To Prevent a War, Break the Russiagate Coup

faced fraud, simply denied.[10]

I came to that view of Euler's fully witting hoax, in his attack on the then long-deceased Leibniz, through my disgust at the teaching of both analytic geometry and the calculus to which I was exposed in both my secondary-school education, and in my attendance at a university, later. I could never bring myself, formally or morally, to pollute my mind with belief in the empiricist rubbish which I was instructed to believe on those occasions. This rejection of such instruction turned out to be a source of my most important margin of intellectual advantage over my putative professional rivals among the economists of the recent half-century to date.

What saved me from the mistakes of my more important rivals among economists, has been, first of all, the influence of Gottfried Leibniz on me from about the age of 14-15, and, later, since my embrace, by January-February 1953, of, principally, Bernhard Riemann's work, his 1854 habilitation dissertation, most emphatically.

Thus, today, if any good outcome is to occur during the presently onrushing general physical-economic breakdown-crisis of the world as a whole presently, this can only occur through the influence of those same principles which I have adopted in the course of my unique successes as an economic forecaster during the recent half-century.

This involves what must be considered, under present circumstances, as a specific, unique conception of the nature of the power of creativity encountered in the characteristic potential of the human individual mind expressed by discovery of universal principles of experiment. This is the immediate subject here, the subject on which the urgently needed adoption of a competent notion of principles of physical economy now depends. The "great experiment" on which the desired achievements depend, is found in the examination of the nature of the efficiently creative powers of the individual human mind.

I illustrate the point, by beginning with a relevant restatement of the nature of the evidence toward which I have just pointed here.

My Own Outlook Was Situated So

My earlier conscious awareness of the crucial issue underlying my account in such locations as here, today, dates, essentially, in beginnings identified with my first encounter with secondary-school teaching of plane geometry. As I have written of this on sundry, relevant occasions, I had rejected the *a-priori* assumptions flatly at first encounter, asserting my belief, then, that only a *physical* geometry of the type relevant to design of supporting iron or steel materials crafted to optimize mass and strength according to structural forms, represented a true geometry.[11] Once the subject of construction was freed from the illusions of Euclidean geometry by attention to the physical principles of design of forms of construction, the absurdity of Euclid's mis-interpretation of the achievements of those forerunners from among the Pythagoreans and Platonics, became immediately as obvious as Riemann insisted to be the case, as in the opening paragraphs of his 1854 habilitation dissertation.

So, from that date during my early adolescence, on, all of my subsequent exposure to instruction in secondary education and as much higher education as I could tolerate, placed me in opposition to the underlying presumptions of almost everything in, or about the method for science thus presented to me in those classroom environments, at those times.

Satan and His Monetarism

All standard teaching of modern economics dogma has been premised on the misguided presumption, that the appropriate assignment of a notion of relative economic value was a statistical-monetary function: *monetarism*. To understand that prevalent error of classroom and related opinion, and, thus, the practical consequences of the existing of the present world monetary form of general breakdown-crisis of all among the present world monetary systems, we must consider the following typical aspects of the history of this phenomenon of globally extended European culture today.

This notion is traced in European history since the period of the Peloponnesian War, with the reign over European and extended civilizations by monetarist imperial powers of the type associated with the functions of the treasuries located under the direction of the Delphi cult of Apollo-Dionysos.

___
10. All of those Eighteenth and early Nineteenth centuries' Leibniz-haters among the followers of Paolo Sarpi's cult of empiricism commit a fraud kindred to that of such Nineteenth-century cases as Laplace and his three-body problem, Laplace's protégé Cauchy, and the hoaxsters Rudolf Clausius and Hermann Grassmann. The fraud against the work of Wilhelm Weber by Clausius and Grassmann, is typical.

___
11. A conclusion I had reached through study of construction in progress as Boston's Charlestown U.S. Navy Yard prior to that time.

The failure of the propagators of the warfare among Athens, Corinth, and Syracuse, created what Plato treated as the opportunity for what had been envisioned by him as the opportunity to consolidate the salutary destruction of the temporarily failed maritime-monetary power of the Delphi Apollo-Dionysos cult during that time. The later establishment of the Roman Empire, through the negotiations conducted between the figure who was to become known as Augustus Caesar in negotiations with the Isle of Capri-based representatives of the priesthood of the Mithra cult, did establish a Mediterranean-based form of maritime-based, single monetarist imperialism, a Roman empire still dominated by the Delphi cult since a point through, and beyond the lifetime of the last leading priest of that cult, the notorious, typically Delphic, illustrious liar Plutarch. That imperialism, in its subsequent incarnations in sundry kaleidoscopic expressions, has been the imperial monetarist system which has reigned over Europe most of the time, since that time, a monetarist empire of which the Anglo-Dutch monetarist imperialism is the world-dominating expression at the present time.

Contrary to the fables of monetarism,, the ruling principles respecting the determination of effective value, lie within the bounds of a needed science of physical economy, not the statistical habits of intrinsically imperialist monetarist systems.

Essentially, from its beginnings in such places as 1620-1687 Massachusetts, the design of the American System of political-economy, on which the United States' republic was premised, has been based on a credit system, rather than a monetary system, Alexander Hamilton's particular genius in defining the American System of political-economy as a remedy for the bankruptcy of the separate banking systems of the thirteen former colonies, required, and established that Constitutional reform of a constitutional republic, rather than a confederation, a sovereign republic whose existence was indispensable for saving an otherwise bankrupt, new nation-state.

It was this same principle of our Constitution, which was employed by President Abraham Lincoln to defeat

From the beginnings of the United States, in the Massachusetts Bay colony, there was a commitment to a credit system, in the interest of technological progress. Here is a reconstruction of the Saugus Iron Works, in Massachusetts, which were built in the mid-17th Century.

the otherwise victorious British imperial power behind both the slaveholders' secession and the London-owned New York bankers, through the system of "greenbacks" which was organically integral to the great principle of physical economy on which the creation of the U.S. Federal Constitution was premised.

This must be said, to make clear the impossibility of any continuation of civilization on this planet without eliminating all monetarist authority and monetarist systems. The action required is to establish a planetary system based on a fixed-exchange-rate credit-system among a leading set of the aggregately powerful nation-states of the planet, to the effect of putting all monetary systems out of existence. This reform must employ a credit-system as a medium designed, and managed, all to the effect of creating a system of international credit, that based on a principle of fixed-exchange-rate lending among the participating sovereign states of the planet.

This measure solves the immediate problem of global bankruptcy among all nations presently, but it also poses the need to take the matter of policy of credit and prices out of the domain of "free trade" monetarism—or anything like it, thus posing the issues of physical-economic values, rather than the merely nominal, and usually more or less badly mistaken notions of relative monetary prices. The Hamiltonian form of constitutional model of the U.S. Constitution, serves as the needed linchpin for establishing the pattern of global, long-term credit-agreements among a dominant set of initiating nations composing the kernel of the new world physical-economic system.

What are the chances of establishing such a system now? The only force which exists to bring this change about, is that no nation of the planet has any rational chance of surviving the presently wildly escalating crisis, without accepting that reform. That is the looming breakdown-crisis being brought on rapidly, now, by the miscreations called the British empire and its pro-fascist-like puppet, the Obama administration, whose self-inflicted folly will present what I have proposed as the only available opportunity for surviving the presently onrushing, global breakdown-crisis.

Do the Anglo-Dutch Liberal oligarchs know this? Of course they do: much better than you do. Nonetheless, their inherently self-doomed system is the only world system under which they are presently disposed to live. Their impulse is either to win, or to bring down all nations of the world, like the fabled Cities of the Plain, rather than accept the existence of any world system but their own. Therefore, foolish Obama as been chosen as their silly tool.

Where I Stand

On that account, I have paid a certain price, from adolescence to the present day, for my resistance to what I was presumably being ordered to comply with in these matters; but, then, experience, since that time, has demonstrated, that those of my contemporaries who accepted what I had resisted, paid a fearful price for what they had lost from their own creative powers, that by accepting the damaging, axiomatic and kindred beliefs which I had the good fortune to have rightly rejected. So, we have the fact that virtually every putatively leading economist, even among the relatively best, has failed in precisely those crucial aspects of forecasting in which my successes have been unique, the fact which illustrates the point.

Now, on the happier side of such matters, the truly intelligent professionals in the field of economy will be inclined, increasingly, to collaborate with me in bringing about the needed measures to save our republic, in particular, and the rest of the nations as well. Once the principle of the matter is made clear to them, many among them will discover, already lurking within themselves, what is otherwise needed to make them adequate to carry out the remainder of the task.

Recently, since, most notably, the aftermath of my July 25, 2007 forecast of the imminence of the general breakdown-crisis, my relations with leading U.S. and other economists have been significantly improved. Such has been the effect of the forecast which I presented in an international webcast, brought forth on that occasion. However, while the importance of my unique contribution has become appreciated, more and more, among competent professionals, the essential reasons for the success of my own record as a forecaster over recent decades, has not yet been grasped adequately even among the relatively best of those among what might be termed my "relevant peers." It is thus, my obligation, as here, to improve this state of affairs, which is prominent among the motives for publishing what I now write on that account.

Therefore, to recapitulate what I had just written as the opening of the present chapter: what saved me from the mistakes of my more important rivals among economists, has been, first of all, the influence, as I have already restated here, of Gottfried Leibniz on me, from about the age of 14-15, and, later, since my embrace of it, by January-February 1953, principally, Bernhard Riemann's work, his 1854 habilitation dissertation, most emphatically.[12] Such were the indispensable preconditions for all of my own original discoveries represented by my relevant contributions reshaping the national and world economic policies to be considered here.

There has been nothing accidental in the outcome of those differences in adopted belief respecting matters of science bearing upon the subject of a science of physical economy. This is the case, most notably, in the domain of, principally, medium to long-range economic forecasting. There has been nothing actually obscure, or accidental in my successes, nor, my putative professional rivals' failures on this account.

It is not accidental, that my accomplishments have all been situated within the framework of my studies

------

12. While the act of a discovery of anything approaching a discovery of a true universal principle is an act by an individual person, it would be a serious mistake in method to imagine that a valid discovery of principle by a person means that the development and outcome of that discovery is an isolable, individual action. Here, the principle of dynamics (or, the ancient concept of *dynamis*) must be taken into account. The development of knowledge of true principles is an ongoing process of development of each idea, which occurs through the participating role of contributors to such a process of discovery. History is not a sequence of events, but a process of the self-development of the minds of the successive persons and generations which, in effect, transforms the characteristics of the mental life of successive generations.

and development within the domain of a science of physical economy. On that account, the following clarification is crucial.

Physical Economy is The Human Science

The root of the failure of the modern European economists and their American followers, as distinct from the patriotic American school of Benjamin Franklin and Alexander Hamilton, is essentially the fact, that the establishment of the imperial Anglo-Dutch supremacy of the British East India Company's Lord Shelburne, since the February 1763 Peace of Paris, put continental Europe, increasingly, under the tyranny of the economic policies associated with that "Liberal"school of John Locke, Adam Smith, and Jeremy Bentham, an Eighteenth-century school[13] which

Improvements in productivity depend upon an increase in the energy-flux-density of physical economic processes, per capita and per square kilometer. This points to the indispensability of nuclear power, for human survival and progress.

had been formed under the persisting influence of Paolo Sarpi, and of Sarpi's adoption of the methods of the medieval irrationalism of William of Ockham.

Ockham is the founder of the specific form of moral corruption and fervid irrationalism of the modern Anglo-Dutch Liberalism. The most evil man of the Twentieth Century, Sarpi follower, and anti-science fanatic, and devoted hater of mankind, Bertrand Russell, serves as an epitome, still today, of everything that is most essentially evil in the world at large.

The prevalent dogma in European culture since the rise of the Liberalism of Paolo Sarpi et al., has been the presumption, as by Adam Smith, in his 1759 **Theory of Moral Sentiments**, that no actual universal physical principles exist within the bounds of mankind's actual knowledge, but only rules of behavior consistent with the lack of any recognized universal principles, but only those of what is, presumably, merely custom. The moral depravity of those advocates of "Behaviorist economics" associated with the conspicuously pro-fascist, even pro-Nazi, health-care and other current economic policies of the President Obama administration's health care and social policies, are typical of the relatively worst outcome produced by driving the evil dogmas of John Locke, Adam Smith, and Jeremy Bentham to their Nazi-like extremes.

Essentially, protests against naming President Obama's economic policies as either "Hitler-like," or, simply, "Nazi," are behavior tantamount to intellectual and moral complicity in a great crime against humanity. It is the wild-eyed hoax of "cap and trade" and all, in the present Summer of American cooling, which is a new cloak for, a carbon copy of Hitler's own policies of genocide.

Hence, for today's consistent followers of the tradition of Locke, Adam Smith, and Bentham in the field of economy, a field in which I play a starring role of opposition to their legacy presently, for them, economic processes express no actual principles, but only conventions based on adopted customs of belief chosen without regard to any actually efficient universal physical principles. Hence, we have the case of the influence of widespread, intrinsically incompetent methods of so-called statistical forecasting more widely. Whereas, my own forecasts have been specifically successful, virtually all rivals, of all persuasions in the field, have been systemically failures as forecasters on this account.

Ironically, it is exactly their beliefs to this effect, which have served as the instrument of destruction of

---

13. Locke died in A.D. 1704, but his influence permeated the British imperialist dogma to the present day inside the U.S.A.

all civilization which is the oncoming menace overtaking the entire planet today. Such are those particular "behaviorist" beliefs of the Obama administration which has put the U.S. republic on the chutes to Hell right now.

For Example:

It is fairly said, that productivity increases with both the amount of the power supplied to production and integrally related activity, and also the increase of what is termed the energy-flux-density of the physical economic processes, per capita and per square kilometer. Any effort either to allow those "energy" values to decline, or even to fail to increase, per capita and per square kilometer, spells an oncoming relative, or more severe disaster, such as the world in general has been suffering, with increasing severity, since about September 2007, but, actually, since about March 1, 1968.

This present influenza pandemic is only a marker for the far more destructive conditions which will become rampant unless the present directions in, most notably, U.K. and U.S.A. economic and social policies, are sharply reversed, and, in large part, uprooted and destroyed together with all relics of monetarism as such.

Thus, in that sense of the currently plummeting world economies, there never will be a recovery from the general, physical breakdown which will continue to be spreading without interruption, as since about September 2007, spreading, and worsening at a presently accelerated rate, in each and every nation of this planet. This will continue either for as long as the presently dominant policy-shaping of the imperial United Kingdom and its present puppet President Barack Obama remain in charge, or until the system of nations of the world as a whole has simply died for failure to terminate the present trends in policy-making by the Obama Presidency, now, or during some early days ahead.

Without the very early and widespread reversal of the policies to which those failed regimes in Britain and elsewhere are most passionately devoted at this time, there never will be a recovery of the human race from an accelerating breakdown crisis presently in progress—not until after the present collapse of civilization, globally, had long since struck bottom.

Thus, with that crucially important qualification taken into account, the presently ongoing breakdown of the imperial-London-steered entirety of civilization, would lead, at the best, to an already very steep dive, still accelerating into a general, planetary new dark age

for the human species as a whole. The stated intention of Britain's Prince Philip, and of his World Wildlife Fund, to employ measures intended to bring about a rapid collapse of the human living population from an earlier approach to seven billions persons soon, to less than two, is the current policy of a widely reigning, intentionally genocidal cult-doctrine called, variously, "globalization," or "cap and trade."

The cause for these man-made crises, is not "natural" in any appropriate sense of that term. They are the fruit of entirely man-made, essentially, criminally insane policies, policies which have been adopted by all-too-powerful oligarchical forces of monetarist rule predominating in the policy-shaping of the combined efforts of the most powerful nations and monetarist interests today.

As in the particular case of the present so-called "health care" policies of the Obama Administration, this onrushing general breakdown-crisis of all mankind is the fruit of psychopathological policies whose influence over the planet is centered jointly in the globally imperial British monetary authority and its most significant puppet, the "Nero-like" President Barack Obama Administration of today.

This brings us now to a most crucial, leading point.

Human Creativity: The Mind

In the recently issued **Economic Science, in Short**, I have featured a summary identification of those principal features of the human mental-perceptual processes, which, when taken into account as a whole process, represent the resources on which competent economic practice now urgently depends. There, I describe, in a fresh, more valid way than generally available from other professional sources today, the related, essential distinction between the human mind, on the one side, and the behavior of all lower forms of life, on the other. That is the specific topic here, on which the attention of this present element of this report as a whole is focused.

As I have written or spoken on earlier occasions: what has been presently treated, heretofore, as physical science, has been devoted, chiefly, to society's reading of the bodies of evidence specifically limited to those subjects of non-living and living processes which have been examined on the presumption, that mankind's view of these processes is, at it is said, "objective." What has been customarily presumed to have been the proper subject of the physical science of man's own

Rembrandt van Rijn was dedicated to portraying the proper subject of science, man's actual state of mind. This 1659 self-portrait is an example.

part, man's actual mental behavior, has been wrongly defined as what continues to be a generally presumed notion of "physical objectivity." In that misguided, but commonplace approach, the actually crucial, *subjective* aspect has been essentially excluded from consideration, as if *a-priori*, in favor of what has been wrongly presumed to have been physical science's *objective* application to both non-living and living processes.

Men and women may have chosen their actions, but what higher power than mere sense-perception, shaped their decision?

The fact underlying those decisions which have misled the world into the presently onrushing, general breakdown-crisis, is, that the world in its entirety, is presently within the grip of a plausibly terminal state of a general breakdown-crisis of all existing societies. Were there no appropriately radical overthrow of the patterns of decision-making responsible for the recent habits of government, respecting economy in particular, humanity as a whole were presently self-condemned to a calamity far beyond any known in the past experience of mankind as a whole.

Vastly genocidal crises, such as those which any continuation of the present trend in policies of both the United Kingdom and the Barack Obama administration portends, had already struck limited portions of humanity as a whole, in different parts, in earlier times. However, this present crisis is the first known case in which it is the entirety of the human species which is known to be threatened so, a threat of a kind arising globally from the effects of applying bad policies globally, policies made by the most influential bodies of opinion-making, brought so savagely, upon the planet as a whole, in what is intended by today's London-centered imperialists for our planet in its entirety.

Yet, there is nothing about this onrushing threat of early doom which should be considered mysterious to sane and well informed minds. The doom now hurtling in its descent upon our entire planet, is not an inevitable consequence, but a willfully chosen result by the monetarist relative few, who are currently reigning over the prevalent political-economic systems of the planet's few most powerful nations and the intrinsically monetarist imperial cabals within which those nations are situated.

That specific, relevant moral and also practical folly in the susceptibility of the apparently prevalent human nature of every part of society throughout the planet presently, resides essentially in a practiced misconception of human nature itself. The most notable aspects of this pattern of self-destruction of the U.S.A. and virtually all other leading nations of the planet generally, have been essentially psychological in form in their causes, but no less physical in their consequences.

The most significant of those presumptions governing the psychology of evil presently permeating political-economy and related subjects, is what is known presently as the empiricist method of Anglo-Dutch Liberalism, or, what is named otherwise as a Satanic cult of "filthy lucre," otherwise known euphemistically as "monetarism," or, simply, the "philosophical Liberalism" misconceived in the Ockhamite irrationalism of the followers of the "new Venice's" Paolo Sarpi. Such is the so-called Anglo-Dutch monetarists' Liberal imperium typified by the intrinsically irrationalist dogma of such as John Locke, Adam Smith, and Jeremy Bentham.

That doctrine and practice of "Liberalism," is to be treated as a potentially mass-murderous, pandemic mental disease of the present world monetary system, a pathogen infecting the popular human mind, a conceit through whose assistance all other sorts of diseases afflicting humanity find and take their advantage.

How the Horror Prevailed

It is the efficiently physical character of the *dynamic*[14] processes which regulate the relevant patterns of mass behavior of the human individual minds, which is the key to understanding the how and why of the presently onrushing general economic and demographic breakdown-crisis of the entirety of this planet as a whole at this time. To remedy this "lemming-like" behavior of the rulers of nations generally today, we must examine the relevant, potentially fatal factors of opinion which have allowed the present great folly to have been unloosed upon the entirety of mankind, as this occurred in the aftermath of the inauguration of the Winston Churchill-loving, U.S. President Harry S Truman, on April 13, 1945. We must get to the root of the matter, thus echoing a most crucial point already made in my **Economic Science, in Short**.

Essentially, generally speaking, mankind, through the dying out of the generations which arose to fight the Hitler regime, does not presently know, or even remember, the principles which actually misgovern and, thus, mislead, the individuals' own mind, that to such effect as the toleration of the swindle which the British empire has imposed upon the U.S.A. through a British monarchy puppet, a caricature of the narcissistic Roman Emperor Nero, a living caricature currently serving as President of the U.S.A.

In particular, we must focus attention on what are to be recognized as the actually creative, and physical processes typical of the healthy individual human mind. It is the failure to grasp the nature of that principle of human creativity associated with Classical artistic and

physical-scientific achievements on which all human progress has depended, which has promoted those effectively insane monetarist and related policies which had created the present conditions for a currently accelerating general physical-economic breakdown-crisis of the entirety of our planet.

It is time that our institutions of government pay closer attention to the respective proper functions and diseases of the popular mind.

The Achievements and Follies of Science

In the first, ordinary case, the individual locates his, or her sense of personal identity more crudely, naively, within the bounds of what is presumed to be a domain of the experience of sense-certainties. In the second, which must prevail now, if civilization is to outlive the present crisis, the creative scientist, or accomplished, actually creative Classical artist, alike, locates his, or her sense of personal identity in reality, by regarding apparent sense-certainty as a mere shadow of that reality which only the actual or potential, scientific or Classical artistic genius tends to recognize as being the real universe.

The case of Johannes Kepler's uniquely original discovery of the principle of universal gravitation, as reported by him in his **The Harmonies of the Worlds**, is an example of the efficiency of what I have indicated as the second, higher choice of self-connection.[15]

For this purpose, Johannes Kepler's uniquely original discovery of the principle of universal gravitation, is unique, in many respects, for competent modern science in general; but, there is one included feature of the method which he employed in the discovery of the principle of gravitation, which is of specific interest at this immediate place in my presentation. That special interest lies in the distinct concept termed "universal physical principle." This is a notion of principle which may be adumbrated by a mathematical formulation, just as Kepler defined the mathematical formulation used to describe a measurable effect of gravitation, but can only be competently derived otherwise. The universal

---

14. Dynamic is used in the sense of Gottfried Leibniz, and of the concluding paragraph of Percy Bysshe Shelley's 1819 **A Defence of Poetry**.

15. The issue of which choice of English translation of the title of this work by Kepler, hangs upon emphasizing, on the one hand, the use of "world" in the sense of the universe as a single object, and, the more practical implication, of "harmonies of the worlds" which reflects the process by which the role of emphasizing harmonics in defining the discovery of universal gravitation in the organization of the worlds. The latter option is the more meaningful one, scientifically.

principle of gravitation *apparently bounds* the physical space-time of our Solar system (and beyond) in a way, a curvature of physical space time which bounds the Solar system, and which defines our universe as finite, and as, in no sense "Euclidean," for that very reason.

However, although it might appear to some that it was by virtue of Kepler's uniquely original discovery of precisely that set of mathematical relations which the circles of silly Sir Isaac Newton claimed, with blatant fraud, as their discovery, that gravitation is the source of the relevant physical power; in fact, the mathematical expression is a shadow cast by the principle itself, not its efficient substance. Hence, we have Einstein's famous formulation of the case of what he recognized as the absolute originality of Kepler's discovery.

All competent modern physical science, since the work by Kepler, has characteristics which, as Albert Einstein emphasized, reflect the specific quality of irony expressed by Kepler's discovery of the principle of gravitation. There is no competence in modern science, except by aid of Einstein's assessment of the essential role of Nicholas of Cusa follower Kepler's discovery for all competent modern science in general. Nonetheless, although this view of Kepler is the standpoint of competent modern science in general, it is also a fact that as Carl F. Gauss showed by his discovery of the orbit of the asteroid Ceres, there are additional complexities of a related quality within physical space-time generally. These complexities began to come clearly into view with that development by Gauss, of what came to be the tool of physical mathematics which came to be known as the tensor, a tensor conceived as a physical-experimental,

Leonardo da Vinci was the quintessential scientific and artistic genius, mastering music, physical science, and other arts. Here are his drawings of the viola organista, *which he invented, and his schematic of a flying machine.*

rather than merely mathematical tool.[16]

I explain the general principle involved in that, as follows.

Kepler's uniquely original discovery of the universal physical principle of Solar-systemic gravitation is, still today, the Classical demonstration of the proper method for defining the proven existence of a true universal physical principle. It is for this reason that Albert Einstein attributed such crucial significance of Kepler's method in any competent expression of modern physical science, still to the end of Einstein's own life. My associates and I have returned, repeatedly, to the "Kepler paradigm;" in my own case, the most frequent motive has been to emphasize the distinction between the misleading definition of a proof of principle under the British empiricist method derived from the Okhamite method of Paolo Sarpi's empiricism, and that contrary method of competent physical science which is shown most efficiently by the case of Kepler's original discovery of universal gravitation, and best illustrated today by the legacy of the Leibniz concept of the efficient character of the "infinitesimal," which is expressed best, currently, by the Riemannian heritage of Albert Einstein and Academician V.I. Vernadsky.

The corresponding question is, typically: what is the physical meaning of the Leibniz infinitesimal? Is that "infinitesimal" a phantom; or, does it represent crucial

---

16. Sky Shields' crafting of his revealing portrait of the method, based on the concept of the tensor, which Gauss had actually employed for his discovery of a series of asteroid orbits, is used as a typical point of reference comparisons, throughout this present report.

evidence of a fatal flaw in what, until now, has passed for an increasingly, generally taught, British version of scientific method of those positivists whose influence is to be traced most specifically in the train of Ernst Mach and Bertrand Russell, and the science-degenerates who have followed them, since, approximately, the closing decades of the Nineteenth Century? This question is key for understanding the actual nature of the truly sane human mind.

III. The Human Mind: Two Views

*In what had been my argument in my **Economic Science, in Short**, I located the quality of true human individual creativity in terms of reference to two, alternate choices of the individual's sense of the "location" of his, or her personal identity. In the more common case, the customary choice was located, mistakenly, in the notion of personal identity associated with the notion of "sense-certainty." In fact, unfortunately, actual human creativity is located in the relatively rarer case, that of the actually creative individual, which is presently rare even among prominent scientists. The source of that problem is, unfortunately, a popular, wrong-headed present tradition of the recent four decades; in truth, creativity, when and where it exists, is located typically in the sense of personal identity which is located, functionally, by a sense of self as located in "a different experience": not within a domain of formal mathematics as such, but, as I have emphasized repeatedly, in earlier locations, in the domain associated with the Classical mode of the poetic imagination, as this is reflected, in Classical English expression, in Percy Bysshe Shelley's **A Defence of Poetry**, its closing paragraph, most emphatically*

In fact, however, even in the case of the significantly

Leonardo da Vinci portrayed the individual's "sense of self" as being beyond sense certainty, as shown in his 1490 "Portrait of a Musician."

creative individual personality, the continued presence of the child in the man, is shown by shifts of the visibly expressed sense of personal identity, from the lower of these two locations to the higher, or, the reverse, as this tends to vary with the circumstances, in such cases.[17]

Most notably, scientific creativity, like that of Classical poetic and the Classical musical composition of J.S. Bach, Joseph Haydn, W.A. Mozart, and Beethoven, is excluded in a systemic way, by today's widely prevalent, even reigning, popularized trash entertainments and interpersonal social conduct. Actual expressions of creativity, are not located within the confines of mathematics, but are typified by Classical modes of creative processes specific to Classical artistic composition, Classical poetry most emphatically. The ironical fact of the matter is, that the best scientists of the Nineteenth and Twentieth centuries were often also qualified, like Albert Einstein, as Classical musicians, even if as amateur performers; the decline in Classical musical participation has crucial relevance for understanding the relative collapse of scientific competence shown among generations born post-World War II, among all but a few exceptional minds from among the younger generations living today. My own organization of

---

17. The reference to the failings among even today's "leading scientists," reflects the accelerated down-shift of the ratio of actually productive members of the potentially total labor-force, in Europe as in North America, this as a consequence of the collapse of net levels of basic economic infrastructure in the U.S.A., in particular, since 1967-68, as this has been combined with a related decline in the ration of farmers, industrial operatives, (actual) scientific workers, and engineering and related labor, within the labor-force. The employed members of the labor-force had been, increasingly, persons employed in "make-work" of doubtful physical-economic and related value. Thus, the base-line role of actual science in employment, has declined, at the same time that pseudo-scientific personnel have been counted as part of the labor-force. Thus, there has been the loss of a science-driver mission, even merely technical competence, within the population generally.

a young-adult organization, with emphasis on Classical-artistic and scientific emphasis at the same time, reflects my strategic commitment to promoting insight into this crucial role of Classical artistic culture in providing the conditions required for promoting the development of a kernel of the promising young-adult intellects in any serious profession today.

This central role of Classical art in generating the creative powers of imagination, when it is permitted to work to such effect, has wonderful implications for the good.

At the same time, the post-1945 moral degeneracy in trans-Atlantic European culture, as under the influence of existentialism generally, and the ·European Congress for Cultural Freedom (CCF), in particular, typifies the way in which the post-war cultural degeneration in Classical music has led in shaping a morally downward pattern of post-World War II cultural, moral, and economic degeneration, as among the principal causes for the currently prevalent moral, intellectual, and economic decay, and the presently threatened, early doom, of globally extended European culture.

When the proverbial "smoke has cleared" from the learning of the most crucial point in both my preceding **Economic Science, in Short**, and this present sequel, the most crucial point which I present in both instances, is my insistence that competent science depends upon recognizing that *the location of the human individual's power to discover a valid principle, the noëtic power, is to be found in the domain of the best examples from Classical poetry and related artistic compositions, rather than in the language of mere mathematics.* The evidence which supports that conclusion, is both systemic in nature, and is clear enough in itself, but that is so only when the relevant point, which I made in that earlier writing, is taken into account, as I do, more fully, in the following pages, here.

As I emphasized in that earlier piece, the key to presenting a proof of that distinction, begins with the thinker's self-critical reflection on the ironical relationship posed by considering a particular phenomenon from the vantage-point of the contrast of the same subject-matter, when, on the one hand, the emphasis is shifted from one sense of the "location" of personal identity, the ordinary, popular choice, to the higher, as this higher viewpoint is typified by Johannes Kepler's uniquely original discovery of universal gravitation, in which what was crucial has been his contrast of a mental image of the orbital system based on extension of a notion of visible space, to the contrasting one of harmonics.[18]

The specific type of problem, which should provoke some preliminary insight into the very specifically human nature of true human creativity, is what is otherwise expressed by Gottfried Leibniz's long struggle in his efforts to perfect his uniquely original discovery of the part played by what is ostensibly the "mathematical infinitesimal" in his discovery of the calculus.[19] Once certain elementary facts of the matter are duly considered, the origin of the ironies of the Leibniz infinitesimal, as within the preceding, unique discoveries of the principle of gravitation by Kepler, is directly clarified. This matter of the two choices of personal sense of identity, the mathematically "nitty-gritty," versus the Classical artistic, is crucial.

In this present report, I reference, and build upon what I wrote on this matter of the two, alternative senses of personal human identity, as I did in my **Economic Science, in Short**. As the reader shall be informed here, from this point on, the entire edifice of a competently defined science of physical economy, depends upon precisely these elementary conceptions which I recapitulate, and amplify, here, as I shall show in the subsequent, concluding chapter of this present report.

The Core Argument

To begin the argument of this point, I repeat, that to the degree that the individual regards the experience of his or her senses as "self-evident," that individual's sense of personal identity is identified, as to content, by the misguided presumption that sense-experiences are the immediate, "hard" reality of the universe. That un-

---

18. The same point is illustrated by the Pythagoreans' emphasis on the importance of the principal forerunner of European science, *Sphaerics*, as is shown by the emphasis on the concept of the "comma."

19. Let no one who is not morally corrupted be so silly as to suggest that foolish Sir Isaac Newton ever actually discovered a calculus, or the principle of gravitation. The very fact, that Eighteenth-century acolytes of defenders of foolish and fraudulent Rene Descartes, such as Abbe Antonio Conti and the absolutely disgusting Voltaire, that the Leibniz infinitesimal pertained to a merely imaginary numbers, as the foolish Abraham de Moivre and D'Alembert did, or as the more witting hoaxster Leonhard Euler frankly lied outrightly, opportunistically, on this matter, is that without the actual infinitesimal, there is no actual calculus, but only the simple-minded infinite series taught to Newton by his puppet-masters. The evidence is a matter of rather simple facts. My conclusion is that Euler, like many "politically conscious" opportunists of science today, was, as different evidence shows, too intelligent to believe a single word he said on the subject of the Leibniz infinitesimal, but too career-conscious to tell the truth at that, or even a later time.

fortunate individual, thus defines the notion of "self," accordingly. So, the victim of that adopted illusion defines "devotion to the alleged facts" of the eyewitness experience, and of its associated senses of relative pleasures and pains. Such is the implication of the both morally and clinically pathological mental state of the so-called "behaviorists" of the Anglo-Dutch Liberals' sexual persuasion. Such were the actual, or should-be patients of Dr. Sigmund Freud.

Similarly, as in the attempted mastery of Classical musical aptitudes in the J.S. Bach tradition, even technically skilled musicians fail to reach the goals of the modern Classical musical tradition of Bach through Brahms, not because they do not know how to sing, or perform instrumental works, but because they have failed to comprehend what should have been, for them, the relevant purpose of that mission. In the cases of such short-comings, they may appear to succeed (almost) technically, but fail to reach the appropriate goal of the mission artistically. They fail to grasp true artistic creativity in their efforts to locate their personal identity in the necessary choice of place.

So, the outlook of the great Classical-artistic minds, such as those of the Platonic tradition, or the Apostle Paul of I **Corinthians** 13, and the actually qualified scientific thinkers, is directly contrary to that of both the naively reductionist and the scoundrels from the ranks of the Liberal followers of Paolo Sarpi and his adopted William of Ockham. The Apostle Paul, writing there, sees the world of sense-experience as if in a darkened mirror, or through a murky glass pane: *as if at a distance from the sensed experience from that reality of the universe which is poorly reflected by one's sense-impressions.* Thus, the great scientific thinkers think as the Apostle Paul expresses this, thus, by locating reality in the state of mind which sees sense-experiences as if but shadows of reality, rather than being considered efficient reality as such. Here lies the readily accessible concept of the existence of the human identity in the "soul," rather than the animal husk which that soul, resident essentially in V.I. Vernadsky's Noösphere, temporarily inhabits as its incarnate vehicle for its action within the mortal frames of the sensory domain.

Hence the extraordinary power lodged within the liturgical works of the greatest Classical composers, such as J.S. Bach and such among the continuation of his profession as Haydn, Mozart, Beethoven, Schubert, Mendelssohn. Schumann, and Brahms. The effort to bring the immortality of the human soul actually on

Frans Hals demonstrated that human identity, and creativity, are developed through social interaction, in his painting of St. Matthew reading to a child.

stage, points to the element of sacredness of all great Classical musical composition of the Handel, Bach, Mozart, Beethoven, Schubert tradition in both liturgical and profane compositions. So, for many errant offspring of European civilization, when they lost their connection to the Classical tradition of Bach, they could no longer find contact with their own souls.[20]

The essential distinction at issue on this point, is, summarily, the following.

The connection of the actually human personality to the sensory domain, is provided by the passions which inform human sensual, mortal practice. Here, in the

---

20. Hence, my expressed anger at hearing Lotte Lehmann's artistically slovenly coaching of the tenor performing Florestan's dungeon aria-monologue under her direction. Beethoven's intention in bringing the unfolding of the musical drama to that point was degraded to the purpose of transforming a sublime turning point in that opera into a disgusting moment, as a form of an existentialist travesty. The relationship between secular actualities and the immortality of the soul within a simultaneity of eternity which is the reference point of all Classical artistic work, is the domain of true artistic and related human creativity, as the Apostle Paul's I **Corinthians** 13 is to be referenced on this account.

consequences of those passions, we meet that strife of good against evils of that sort which the presently depraved state of the Obama Administration expresses, in such morbid forms as its frankly evil "health-care" and "cap-and-trade" advocacies. *Let us agree to interpolate, at this point, that it is the humanist passions, such as dedication to the sacredness of the full life of the living human individual, and of the Classical artistic domain, which supply the motive for that creativity on which the morality of actual scientific creativity, among other essential qualities, depends.* Classical modes in poetry, and related elements of song benefitting the crucial contribution to counterpoint of Johann Sebastian Bach, are, thus, among the most nearly perfect expression of those ordered passions of the sublime, as this was typified most neatly by Ludwig van Beethoven's Opus 132 quartet, which have been attained by known civilizations thus far.[21]

In none of what I have just presented in this chapter thus far, is there anything which deserves the epithet, "speculative." The very conception of physical science hangs upon the demonstrable reign over the causal sequence of events, by what are truly universal principles, principles which exist in a demonstrable form which is, in itself, not sensed by the sense-impressions experienced as such, but expressed only in a demonstrably efficient form which lies in a domain which is seemingly external to sense-certainty as such. Despite all

empiricists, the universal principle of gravitation adduced, with unique originality, by Johannes Kepler, exists very efficiently to the present day, despite the efforts to degrade that great universal principle to a dirty empiricist's mere mathematical formula.

Admittedly, certain well-known Jewish and Christian traditions, for example, have failed miserably, as Philo of Alexandria warned the Jewish rabbis of his time against the evils of Aristotle. The Messiah will not consent to appear according to someone's concocted railway time-table. The doctrine of patient submission to evil, was not the mission of the apostles Paul and John, for example. It is not the humble acceptance of degradation, as one were a peaceful serf of one's landlord, which was ever honest Christianity, or the intent of the Mosaic testament of **Genesis** 1. Some say they are Christians, but worship at the Delphi shrine of the Olympian Zeus, thus, in their pitiable, serf-like humility, they deny, in that way, the very existence of that human soul which they claim to treasure.

Now, these necessary things thus said, we are ready to prepare our fresh excursion into the matter of true human individual creativity.

The general consequence of this fact, is that the available sense of personal identity presents the conscious person with two distinct options. Nothing illustrates this better, than examining the case of the empirical distinction among the three known qualities of Earthly existence of mankind: the respective experiences of the *abiotic*, the *Biosphere*, and the *Noösphere*. One of these two options, is the naive notion of simple, mistaken "sense-certainty." Another, is that notion of the intellect of science and Classical art, an intellect which resides at the home address of those discoverable ideas of universal principle which show us the governing principles of the real universe, as principles. Such are the principles of the science of Kepler, Leibniz, Riemann, Einstein, and Vernadsky, as these are distinct ideas, which are expressed, not by sense-experience as such, but which are associated with the powers, such as gravitation, as discovered by Kepler, which are exerted efficiently by what lies in what seems, to the illiterate, to be a mere shadow-world beyond the direct detection of sense-certainties.

Therefore, of which domain have you chosen to be an inhabitant? As a dweller in the mere shadow-land of bare sense-perceptions, or a citizen of the domain within which universal principles rule over the mere shadow-land of sense-perceptions? Thus, you each

---

21. For this insight into the Opus 132, among the late Beethoven package of late string quartets and their by-products, from Opus 127 through 135, I must acknowledge the marvelous contribution to my insights by the celebrated primarius, Norbert Brainin, of the Amadeus Quartet. Our association began during the late 1970s, when he reacted to a Paris distribution of my public protest against the horrifyingly Romantic misinterpretation, under Lotte Lehmann's direction, of Beethoven's Florestan aria opening the second act of **Fidelio**. We met as a result, and soon became fast friends and collaborators. Later, when the Amadeus Quartet was to perform in honor of my 1987, sixty-fifth birthday, the sudden death of the violist Peter Shidlof, not only cancelled that appearance by the quartet, but, most notably, prompted the termination of the contract for the recording and intended pressing, of the new, then on-going series of performances of the complete Beethoven quartet cycle. Beethoven's intent in that composition is, typically, crafted from the standpoint of the real passions of human existence, which lie in the dream-like domain of the soul, seeking to impart a sense of the meaning of those shadows which the soul's reality casts upon the sensory domain. The emblematic fact about this termination of the intended publication of the new series, is that we lost the fresh view of the performance of the Opus 132 which, from my own discussions with Norbert Brainin, would have been a revolutionary advance in depth of insight over all extant performances of that work to the present day. Maestro Brainin's later death was a great loss to humanity, even on this account alone.

have a choice between something which is virtually a mere talking ape, such as President Obama's retinue of "behaviorists" gathered around Timothy Geithner, Larry Summers, and Peter Orszag, or the alternative, of a truly human individual expressing the soul's passion, while in his manifestation in the flesh.

This set of considerations, as I shall show at a later point here, has a decisive impact on the competence, or lack of competence of thinking by nations, including their economic thinking, on the subject of a choice between a failed, and a potentially successful economic policy of nations, both individually, and interacting, today.

A Being of Two Minds

Now, review the most crucial among the points which I developed in **Economic Science, in short**.

In the simpler case, the human individual, and his, or her culture, mimics the beasts as such, perhaps the apes most notably. Such behavior is implicitly premised, largely, on virtually "pre-programmed" control of behavior by sense-perceptions. Otherwise, man is not an ape, and certainly not what might have been a creature designed in the bowels of "Silicon Valley." No higher ape could increase its species' potential relative population-density *willfully*, as humanity does, and that virtually universally. Yet, there is a crucial difference between a society dominated by sense-perceptual knowledge, and a society driven by those forms of fundamental scientific and related cultural progress which defy the prohibitions of the Olympian Zeus of Aeschylus' **Prometheus Bound**. It is the Promethean form of human culture, as affirmed in **Genesis** 1, which expresses the human nature of our species in its most nearly natural form.

Transoceanic navigation developed by regard for the millennia-long, or longer astronomical cycles, is, perhaps, the most typical expression of the task-oriented creativity, when this is considered as a relevant example of a relatively natural state of human culture in the human species, as found in traces of the wisdom developed by very ancient maritime cultures.

As the previous high-point of glaciation retreated, temporarily, despite the global cooling periods such as that which our planet is experiencing now, in the other times when the oceans and seas grew as the ocean waters of the world rose by about four hundred feet, transoceanic maritime cultures moved inland, up what were, initially giant rivers, and gradually settled the territory abutting the riparian flows. Now, as the new upsurge of a fresh "little ice-age" encroaches on our societies today,[22] the same urge which produced the progress of mankind under the reign of the ancient maritime cultures, turns our attention to the other regions of our Solar system, and, also to the larger whole of the galaxy we inhabit, and to the fact of the grip being already exerted on humanity, here, by the radiated effects of gigantic, supragalactic developments beyond.

Much as we men and women of our times, as earlier, prize the form of our mortal existence, it is the outcome of that existence, as we may contribute to that, which is the higher devotion to that which is immortal. What we must come to prize the most in ourselves: are our honor of that past history which has brought us to life, and the legacy we wish to leave behind for vast millennia still to come. These should prompt us to embrace the prospect that there might exist, within the span of the assuredly mortal biological existence of each among us, the prospect that we might contribute to the coming into being of a future more blessed than that we experience now. If we are so inspired, we look within ourselves, searching for a quality within us which could bring forth a future better than that of our own time, and a type of human individual which is a more potent giver of the good than ever before our time.

There, precisely there, we meet the issue of the distinction between available choices of a sense of personal identity.

On the one side, as I had emphasized in my relevant preceding publication, we have the human individual whose sense of being is confined, more or less, to associating his, or her personal identity with what is called, with a certain sense of self-degradation, as the essential dirtiness of sense-certainty. On the other side, there is the nobler form of human consciousness, which regards sense-impressions as merely shadows cast by reality.

This state of two minds is defined by regard for the ironies of the relationship of the creative powers of the individual human to the fictitious world of sense-perception, as I state the case for that, once more, here and now.

As I emphasized this in **Economic Science, in**

---

22. Contrary to liars such as the United Kingdom's Prince Philip, and his flunky and former U.S. Vice-President Albert Gore, there is no present "global warming" syndrome, except in the wicked delusions of the dupes who believe in the pro-genocidal lies of the World Wildlife Fund. The world has already entered an intermediate phase of clearly defined "little ice-age," global cooling.

The beautiful dome on Florence's cathedral, Santa Maria del Fiore, *represents a scientific breakthrough with the use of the catenary curve. A statue of the architect, Filippo Brunelleschi, is in the surrounding plaza, looking up at his achievement.*

Short: on the one side, as I have emphasized in the relevant preceding publication, we have sense-impressions, which are essentially mere "meter readings." These readings are not a direct representation of reality, but are as if shadows cast by each respective sense-organ's activity. If, on the one hand, the individual mistakes these "meter readings" for the real universe, then, he or she locates the efficient existence of his or her own identity in the presumption that what the metering instruments show, is our efficient relationship to the real universe. Call that the nature of sense of identity "A."

If, on the other hand, we accept the evidence that those shadows are just that, merely shadows of reality, then our attachment is to the universe of that reality, an attachment which then situates our sense of personal identity, as not attached to those mere shadows, but with respect to the universe at large: in sense of identity "B ." Then, in the first case, our relationship as a person is to the universe which has cast the shadows chosen by "A" as his or her reality. In the latter option, it is the unseen universe, "B," it is the universe which has cast the shadows called perceptions, which commands our loyalties.

It is the psychological-emotional difference between the notion of one's identity in "A," or "B," as I have addressed this already in **Economic Science, in Short**, which defines the role of human individual creativity in the universe, which defines the subject of Vernadsky's Noösphere. Here we meet the conception of the Leibniz-inspired, Classical European Enlightenment of such as Bach and Friedrich Schiller, as reflected in the concluding paragraph of Percy B. Shelley's **A Defence of Poetry**.[23] Here, we encounter the essential principle of competent physical science and economy.

A Brief Recapitulation

As I have emphasized, repeatedly, in earlier publications over the years, the common principle of all of the leading founders of modern science, including Filippo Brunelleschi as, more emphatically, Nicholas of Cusa, Leonardo da Vinci, Johannes Kepler, Pierre de Fermat, Gottfried Leibniz, and, more recently, Bernhard Riemann and his principal followers Albert Einstein and Academician V.I. Vernadsky,

While the founding principles of a successful mode in modern physical science have been set by the **De Docta Ignorantia** of the crucial Renaissance figure of Cardinal Nicholas of Cusa, there is more than one coin-

---

23. Or the comparable argument of Friedrich Schiller.

cidence between the roles of Brunelleschi and Cusa up through the time of the great ecumenical Council of Florence. The often overlooked, crucial scientific feature of the construction of the dome of the cathedral of Santa Maria del Fiore, as designed and conducted by Brunelleschi, is Brunelleschi's use of the function of the physical principle of the catenary, without which the construction would not have been feasible.

The catenary is a physical curve, sometimes identified as the funicular curve, rather than a formally geometric curve, a physical curve which lies at the center of the most crucial foundations of modern European physical science, including such outcomes as the Leibniz-Jean Bernouilli development of the crucial physical principle of a universal physical principle of least action. The catenary curve's physical properties were explored to crucial scientific effect by the celebrated follower of Cusa, Leonardo da Vinci, who advanced physical science in a functional way by presenting the functional interrelationship of the catenary and tractrix. There is a functional, virtually genetic sort of anti-Euclidean principle connecting this role by Brunelleschi, Cusa, and Leonardo, to both the duplication of the cube by the ancient Archytas and to the fundamental contribution of Bernhard Riemann's own superseding of formal geometries by physical geometry, as in his 1854 habilitation dissertation.

The essential fact of the matter is, that Brunelleschi and Nicholas of Cusa launched the only competent development of modern physical science, the physical science of non-Euclidean physical geometry; their opponents, such as the followers of Aristotle-Euclid and Paolo Sarpi's resurrection of a much-decayed intellectual corpse of William of Ockham, have been failures, often terrible ones, for longer than half a millennium since.

The Crucial Role of Physical Curves

This subject of the distinction between what are to be classed as "naturally" physical curves, such as the catenary, and the formal-geometric curves of the intrinsically, scientifically fraudulent system of Aristotle and his follower Euclid, is of crucial importance for locating a demonstrable sort of experimental form of proof of the true nature of the human mind,

It is important to take into account, in aid of clarity on this point, that Aristotle was a malicious liar, of which it is to be said, as by Philo of Alexandria on theology, that there was no truth, except on subjects such as suitable methods for political assassinations by poisoning,

in the philosophy of Aristotle. My immediate reference here, is to the fraudulent character of the *a-prioristic*, axiomatic presumptions of Euclidean geometry.

The overthrow, by Bernhard Riemann, as in his 1854 habilitation dissertation, of that body of Sophist dogma attributable to the legacy of Aristotle-Euclid in geometry, was the culmination of a long body of resistance to the fraud of Aristotle-Euclid, in the poisonous assumption that physical reality must necessarily proceed from notions of space, time, and matter consistent with the ontological presumptions associated with sense-certainty. The existence of physical geometries which are experimentally real, but which discredit the kind of tradition of a-priorism associated with the Aristotle-Euclid hoax, is not merely the essential root of the quarrel between competent modern scientists and the pagan religious dogmas of the mathematicians, still today; the corresponding types of crucial-experimental physical evidence,[24] show us evidence which is crucial, inasmuch as states of physical processes exist, as typified by the case of the catenary's role in physical scientific subject-matters, which relegate the Aristotle-Euclid arguments to the realms of fairy-tales dwelling only outside the real world.

We had a recent, rather crucial demonstration of this point in the LaRouche Youth Movement basement crew's actual construction of a physical model of the. discovery of the orbit of the asteroid Ceres as the team followed faithfully the construction indicated by the argument by Carl F. Gauss.[25] As the demonstration showed, conclusively, the possibility of Gauss's discovery existed only outside the confines of a pro-Aristotelean sort of a-priorism, in a tensor-space entirely outside the bounds of the Aristotle-Euclid or Newtonian mythologies.

Identity "A" is therefore fictitious; an identity of the type "B," is therefore mandatory, scientifically.

Review the evidence which I have already consid-

---

24. Elementarily physical bio-chemical evidence, such as that associated with the work of William Draper Harkins, V.I. Vernadsky, et al.

25. On the basis of such conclusive experimental evidence, there is no doubt that Gauss was entirely correct in informing Jonas Bolyai et al., that Gauss had already discovered a proof of a true anti-Euclidean physical principle, already during the 1790s, contrary to the weak, failed effort of so-called "non-Euclidean" geometry of Lobatchevsky, et al. Gauss had obviously been prompted by the rejection of Euclid by Gauss's teacher, the great Abraham Kästner, but had gone a step further than presently available records of Kästner's work show. The reconstruction of Gauss's discovery of the Ceres orbit, leaves no further doubt of the relevant connections.

ered in **Economic Science, in Short**, in that light. The fact that the strict interpretation of the case for Euclidean geometry is false relative to the crucial physical-experimental evidence, and that repeatedly, demonstrates that those assumptions based on the *a-prioristic* presumptions of such products of the Aristotle-Euclid presumption, and the modern perversion of that presumption known as empiricism, are intrinsically false to reality. The existence of, and importance of physical curves which are not axiomatically geometrical in origin, provides the key to discovering a true representation of either the universe, or, more modestly, of our practical relationship to it. Such is the "hereditary" implication of the Leibniz-Bernoulli universal physical principle of least action. The evidence supplied by the greatest followers of Bernhard Riemann, such as Einstein and Vernadsky, and, as emphasized by the great Eratosthenes, by the ancient Archytas who duplicated the cube by methods of construction, is crucial.[26]

Identity 'B': The Timely Correction

As I had emphasized in **Economic Science, in Short,** the most crucial evidence of experimental scientific practice, as in my science of physical economy, is, the functions of sense-perception are those of merely shadows of the experienced universe around us. They are neither right nor wrong, except when we make the mistake of blaming them for the wrong interpretations we might often impose upon our experiences. Once we are prepared to presume that these might be merely shadows of reality, rather than a direct view of reality as such, we remain at least relatively sane, and more or less still on firm ground for practice.

As any competent reflections on the work of experimental scientific investigations suggests, we must treat our powers of sense-perception as like any other useful information secured through instrumentation. We must search for mutually contradictory evidence found among the different senses, just as Kepler proceeded in his uniquely original discovery of the principle of universal gravitation ordering the behavior of our Solar system. It is the contradictions among such sources' evidence, on which we are obliged to depend for practicable judgments as to what in our perceptions is illusion, and what is confirmed by examining the conflicting evidence of different specific powers of naturally given, or synthetic modes of sense-perception, as a way to check one type of such information against others.

This means, that, instead of regarding a particular kind of sense-experience as proof of principle, we must explore the contradictory messages of contrasted experience of the same event. In this way, we must reveal to ourselves the principle lurking commonly behind otherwise apparently contradictory, but coinciding experience. The crucial point here, is that the ability to remedy the discrepancies among qualities of sense-impressions, requires an agency which separates and connects the experience (Identity "A") with respect to the identity of the human mind of the individual person (Identity "B").

Thus, the relatively bestialized person believes in what we term "sense-certainty," whereas the actually knowing person is focused upon the means by which relevant kinds of mutually contradictory sensed evidence can be resolved, as if by extended exploratory examinations conducted with the intent of uncovering, in that way, and no other, the nature of the universe (and of its current state) which we inhabit.

However, that observation which I have just introduced, must not be taken simplistically, as if in terms of individual experience as such. Wisdom lies not in individual experience, but in the history of man's interaction with his knowledge of the evolution of experience. In this way, the necessary discipline of the serious thinker, is the need to rise above simple sense-perception of our individual experiences, to a notion which is customarily termed among relevant theologians as a "simultaneity of eternity." In other words, rather than the foolish presumption, that "time," as experienced, contains the universe's actual history as a simple matter of chronology, we must presume what Albert Einstein and others have obliged us to consider as physical-space-time, rather than space and time as qualities presumed to be independent factors defining a fixed framework for our experience.[27]

---

26. Clearly, those who challenge Euclidean geometry only from the inside, are being either intellectually cowardly, or simply incompetent. They, like Lobatchevsky, have employed themselves, at least ostensibly so, in the hopeless quest of challenging their systemically presumed universe, from within the bounds of its own systemically incompetent presumptions. Once we have liberated science from such follies, as Riemann's habilitation dissertation did, we are obliged to rely on crucial-experimental discovery of universal physical principles, as Einstein and Vernadsky have done, rather than hoaxes such as the Aristotle-Euclid concoctions or the followers of the sophist Bertrand Russell in the so-called "Copenhagen School."

27. E.g. Hermann Minkowski's celebrated, 1907 declaration of the end of "time by itself, and space by itself."

The prototypes for the two conceptions of human identity that LaRouche describes— Identity A as bounded by experience, and Identity B as defined by the human mind—are exemplified by the opposing Greek philosophers Aristotle ("A") and Plato ("B").

Such is the difference between the actual historian as a true scientist, of former times, such as my dear friend and collaborator, H. Graham Lowry, and the mere chronologists who have replaced them today.[28] Not that honest chronologists are not invaluable in their own right, but they have usually not grasped the principle of history itself as a scientifically lawful process expressing deep principles of history as in physical science, as my own studies of the physical-economic roots of European culture over the span from ancient Sumer to the present, illustrate. It is the ebbs and flows of the culturally-determined ebbs and flows of increases and decreases of the potential relative population-densities of cultures, peoples, and their nations, which are the true basis for historical physical space-time in the work of the competent historian, a basis which finds its determination in the notion of economy as an expression of ebbs and flows of physical space-time.[29]

These historical flows of cultural processes, supply the basis in evidence for accounting for Percy Bysshe Shelley's theses in his **A Defence of Poetry**. The appropriate subject of our attention in respect to that writing of his, as summarized in the concluding paragraph, is to be recognized as a statement of the same principle of *dynamics* introduced to modern science by Gottfried Leibniz during the decade of the 1690s.

Whereas, the reductionist followers of Paolo Sarpi and Sarpi's lackey Galileo, such as the hoaxster Rene Descartes, present an intrinsically incompetent view of physical science, an incompetent view which presumed the notion proffered to emptied heads by their stupefied admiration of objects floating eternally, in their empty heads, within empty space and time, Leibniz retorted to Descartes' fraudulent scheme, by presenting his revival of the ancient Classical Greek concept of *dynamis*, which has served since as the basis for the only competent modern conception of physical-space-time. Only the stunning opening paragraphs of Bernhard Riemann's 1854 habilitation dissertation, have had a more shockingly profound, and wonderful impact in favor of the progress of science, since the case of Leibniz's presentation of the concept of modern *dynamics*. Only the development of this conception of *Riemannian dynamics* by Albert Einstein and V.I. Vernadsky, has a comparably, deeply underlying, present importance for all mankind today.

The extremely significant implication, for our im-

---

28. H. Graham Lowry, How the Nation Was Won Vol. 1 (Washington, D.C.: EIR, 1987) Graham's second volume was suppressed in the making by, chiefly, two scoundrels, one Fernando Quijano and Quijano's lackey, the opportunist Webster Tarpley. Author (of **Treason in America**) Anton Chaitkin's protest against the fraud by Quijano and Tarpley, then, during 1990-1998, is relevant in this matter.

29. In the case of Anton Chaitkin's work, the title of his principal work, Treason in America, defines, rather exactly, a kind of phase-space demanding further attention by Classical historians.

mediate purposes in this chapter, of the line of argument which I have been presenting in the preceding paragraphs, is the nature and role of the intermediating process which distinguishes the viewpoint of adopted identity "A," from that of identity "B."

The Principle of Experiment

In the naive human creature, sense-certainty, as the fascistic behaviorist lackeys of the Obama administration typify this depraved, "instinctive" moral state of being, reigns over the kingdom of subjects which are the pathetically ignorant. The victim of such a delusion puts himself into a direct, dependent, essentially pagan, morally depraved relationship, to his own senses and appetites, his perceptions of more or less equally gratifying sensations of pleasure and pain. Here we have the case of the type produced by the essential principle of identity "A."

As I have previously emphasized, in sundry places and occasions, the natural, healthy state of development of the individual human personality, prompts that person to despise the conduct, and the opinion of the behaviorist, as that of a victim of his own bestialized depravity. He has no actual morality, but, chiefly, in the final analysis, only the substitute for morality afforded him by his own depraved appetites. It is what he, or she, the narcissist, gets, especially "my own way," rather than the satisfaction in what one is enabled to give, which is the mere mechanism which the hedonist, such as Friedrich Nietzsche, or the utterly depraved Roman Emperor Nero, adopts as a replacement for actually human morality.

The distinction of this depraved individual from the moral person is to be discovered, at least most efficiently, by examining, clinically, the processes of sense-perception. What is the human individual's functional relationship to the system which is his, or her relationship to the experience of sense-perception? It is precisely here, that the functional distinction between type "A" and "B" is most readily located.

It can, and should be said, at this point in the report, that the result of a careful consideration of this question, as to the nature of the difference between the two types, is located in the notion of man and woman as made in the image of the Creator, as defined in **Genesis 1**, or the epistles of such as the Apostles Paul and John.

The brutish person sees sense-perception as immediate reality; type "B" sees the object of sense-perception as a shadowy symptom of the efficient presence of an unseen reality. Not only is what is adduced thus received; but, the receipt prompts a response to the known efficiency of the unseen reality of the universe we inhabit.

So, the relationship of Type "A" to the reality of the same experience, as I defined this distinction in **Economic Science, in Short**, differs absolutely, in principle, from that of Type "B." Type "B" corresponds to the specifically *dynamic*, scientific outlook of such as Leibniz, Riemann, Einstein, and Vernadsky.

Return, for a moment, to a Percy B. Shelley considered from this same vantage-point.

The revolution in that explicit definition of modern physical science supplied, beginning the 1690s, by Gottfried Leibniz, the introduction of the principle of *dynamics*, is to be considered as a notion identical to the thesis presented within the closing paragraph of Shelley's **A Defence of Poetry**:

"The most unfailing herald, companion, and follower of the awakening of a great people to work a beneficial change in opinion or institution, is poetry. At such periods there is an accumulation of the power of communicating intense and impassioned conceptions respecting man and nature. The person in whom this power resides, may often, as far as regards many portions of their nature, have little apparent correspondence with that spirit of good of which they are the ministers. But even whilst they deny and abjure, they are yet compelled to serve, that power which is seated on the throne of their own soul. They measure the circumference and sound the depths of human nature with a comprehensive and all penetrating spirit, and they are themselves perhaps the most astonished at its manifestations, for it is less their spirit than the spirit of the age. Poets are the hierophants of an unapprehended inspiration: the mirrors of the gigantic shadows which futurity casts upon the present; the words which express what they understand not; the trumpets which sing to battle, and feel not what they inspire; the influence which is moved not, but moves. Poets are the unacknowledged legislators of the world."

That passage from Shelley's work is also an echo of the concept of *dynamics* which Leibniz brought to bear against the evil of Descartes.

We are not the particles of which the whole process which we inhabit is composed. We are an expression of that which controls our thoughts and behavior in their effect upon the large, except for those among us who sit above such levels, as those who are qualified to lead societies out of self-inflicted dangers, must exist to do. We who meet that challenge of being representative of Type "B," are the only ones fit to lead society upward out of its own self-inflicted threat of doom, as in the world at large, as now. Such is the social dynamic principle which gives a civilization moral fitness to survive such calamities as grip the world in its entirety at this moment.

Please, therefore, for humanity's sake, now join the ranks of Type "B."

IV. The New Economics

In my earlier professional incarnation as a management consultant, and in my kindred professional functions as an economist, I was often privy to intimate glimpses into the management practices of still functioning firms which were haunted by the memory and other effects of the plausible tycoons who had once led these enterprises, or their like, during the first half of the Twentieth Century and its great economic depression. The generation of their management which I knew personally, was often typified by a blending of surviving sundry heirs and professional managers, who reigned in such firms during the period of my young manhood and later, most among whom were, at their best, pale ghosts of the figures who had formerly led those enterprises.

My direct experience of that sort gave me the advantage of insight into the history and related characteristics of numerous categories of firms comparable to those types I knew more intimately during my own time. There are important lessons to be shared today, to be adduced from my knowledge gained from that time. When I have looked at them, I often recalled the principle of Leibniz's dynamics represented by a passage which I have just cited from what you should recall from the concluding paragraph of Percy Bysshe Shelley's A Defence of Poetry: "The persons in whom this power resides, may often, as far as regards many portions of their nature, have little apparent correspondence with that spirit of good of which they are the ministers. But even whilst they deny and abjure, they are yet compelled to serve, that power which is seated on the throne of their own soul."

In the post-World War II times under the 1945-1953 reign of the unlikely President Harry Truman and his crew, the memory of the President Franklin Roosevelt who had saved us was still powerful to many of us as persons, but his political legacy was already fading in Washington, D.C. itself.

Post-Franklin Roosevelt Wall Street had been in a hurry from the start, hastening to rid the economy and the minds of citizens of almost anything which was a serious reflection of President Franklin Roosevelt's U.S.A.

Essentially, while these enterprises had been something of significance during several decades of earlier time, most notably during the decades preceding the Hoover depression, the managements of those firms, during my encounter with them, were, essentially, living on the laurels, not the intellectual legacy of the deceased late President. It was a time when Wall Street was already in the process of digesting the once respectable, privately held enterprises into a state of oncoming extinction. For that moment, the heirs of the old management enjoyed pretending that they were demigods of entrepreneurial prowess; in reality, they were nothing of the sort. The old pirates, their fading predecessors, even in their kindest moments, would have seen their successors with pity and disgust.

The present managements of my time, during the 1950s and 1960s, assumed that they carried the genes of past economic achievement; but, in fact, they only tried to imitate it, as President John F. Kennedy attempted with some brief successes. There was some remaining, honest skill among the management cadres of such firms, especially the scientists and leading technicians at least, this had been true, at first; but, the system as a whole was already rotting from the top down. Ownership mimicked what it assumed as a style in appropriate postures and imagery, without really understanding anything about the end-result of the post-war process as a whole. Actually, they understood nothing of durable importance respecting the longer term of the economy at large. The ugly years of the Truman Presidency had taken a terrible moral and intellectual toll.

Now, for the most part, those figures from the past, even from most from among my own generation, are now dead in fact. Even the crumbling recollections of what had been the relatively successful management practices of the heirs of the World War II economy, have now become a parody of an abandoned past, a kind of mental, economic wind-up toy which the reigning financier interest of today has no competence in rewinding, with no real actual desire to rewind that which they

The economic policies of President Franklin Delano Roosevelt, shown here talking with a homesteader in North Dakota in 1936, must be revived, if our republic is to be saved.

presume they have inherited as an acquisition gained in the outcome of some shoddy financial swindle led by a Felix Rohatyn or his like. During the late 1970s and 1980s, I also came to know a sampling of some of the best managements in the Federal Republic of Germany; they, too, and their competence, are now chiefly lost in the memories of the past. The utter incompetence in economics matters by the picaresque swindlers of the world since the October 1987 U.S. stock-market crash, has taken over business and related power, but they have no idea of how the damned thing which they had acquired actually ever worked.

Now, especially since the downturn which came approximately March 1, 1968, we have come to far worse times than those of my young manhood of the immediate post-war decades. Even during those decades, we heard chatter about shrewd economic schemes; but, virtually none of the leading present managements of recent decades, has shown even what courtesy might prompt me to identify as respectable competence in management of our nation's economy. Most have become little better than swindlers in the likeness of Enron, of far less than some actual use to anyone, even themselves. Virtually no one in a position of financial potency in finance or management of the shredded remains of infrastructure, agriculture, and industry, actually has the slightest conception of how to go about

bringing our virtually dead economies of the Americas and Europe back to life.

Today, authority and competence have virtually no common ground in either the enterprises or the financial houses and business management schools of today. Only a handful of economists, whose speciality is a serious grounding in recent centuries of history, are likely, these days, to show any actual competence in attempting to fix up the presently, rapidly disintegrating world economy of today.

Presently, the only remaining hope for our republic, and, also, even the world at large, is that the presently accelerating contempt which the Obama Presidency's performance is bringing down upon itself, will bring a qualitative change in the top-most positions of political and private economic leadership, something akin to the Franklin Roosevelt victory brought about in a rather different way all its own.

In the meantime, what has passed for the economic practices of the U.S. Presidencies since March 1, 1968, has been a tried and tested mastery of the art of awful economic incompetence. That fact is the most crucial knowledge which must be brought to the efforts to rescue the world economy from its presently onrushing plunge into a global new dark age today. That is to say, that most of what passes, in today's popular opinion, leading political circles, or otherwise, for competent principles of economic management of either governments or private enterprises, is, like Goldman-Sachs, worse than sham.

Such has become the spirit of this present age.

"Lemonade, anyone?!"

Beginning November 11, 2004, I proposed to relevant circles of the U.S. Democratic Party that the Party pick itself up from the floor of the incredible re-election-victory of the Bush-Cheney ticket, by preparing to defend Social Security against the campaign of rape intended by the pathetic Bush. My proposal was taken up successfully by the Democratic Party during 2005. During that same year, I launched a companion effort to prepare to rescue the massively imperilled U.S. automobile industry. On the latter account, I proposed to assign the portion of the floor-space and personnel no longer required for automobile production, for high-technology-driven programs of building up basic scientific, infrastructure and advanced industrial programs. This latter effort could have worked, but it was sabotaged by Felix Rohatyn and other swindlers in the international financier wings; in February 2006, the U.S.A. abandoned, and destroyed, the U.S. auto industry, which was thus already doomed to experience, under President Obama, what has happened to it now.

What has happened to our nation and its economy, out of a series of disastrous tours through the Bushes, and, now, the made-in-London Obama reign, has been an era ruled by something tantamount to treason, in transforming us into the wreck of the new century, the manifest destruction of our economy and much else under the direction of circles representing London-centered monetarist agencies which have sought to destroy our republic since its emergence, after February 1763, as a force of resistance to the drugs and slavery interests of the emergent world imperialism of Lord Shelburne's British East India Company.

Later, on July 25, 2007, I forecast that immediate breakdown of the U.S. economy into new world depression, the same still oncoming general, global economic breakdown-crisis under which the entire world is virtually dying today. At that time, I proposed the urgently needed action to rescue the remains of the U.S. chartered banking system through reorganization in bankruptcy, while also placing the entire system of mortgaged resident homeowners under bankruptcy protection from foreclosures. During the following weeks, into mid-September, I completed a set of proposals, all based on what I presented in my July 25, 2007 international webcast address; I proposed actions which would have, if adopted, saved the United States, in particular, from all of the ruin which both the U.S. Congress and both George W. Bush, Jr. and Barack Obama have heaped on the U.S.A. and also most of the world, since that time.

In view of the now rapid sinking of the Obama farce, at last, the fresh chance for new leadership of our republic appears to be a bit better than an early possibility that we will get up from the dirt of a Nero-like arena, for one more chance at becoming ourselves once more. However, there is still much that is very grim.

As a result of that particular history, today, the history of the notable combined effects of the measures ac-tually taken by the U.S. Congress and the Presidency, the result has been that the entire world is now plunging, at an accelerating rate, into a general, global breakdown-crisis. This is a crisis which, unless stopped by measures which I have presented, will mean the death of civilization, and perhaps as many as billions of people as a result of the policies which Britain's Prince Philip of the World Wildlife Fund, together with his foolish son and their lackey, former Vice-President Al Gore have proposed. A proposal which those culprits have made in response to an alleged, but non-existent "Global Warming" crisis. The intended destruction of civilization globally is presently intended to occur, beginning immediately, during the great global breakdown-crisis of the period of history immediately ahead. Adolf Hitler would be drooling in envy, were the British owners of their puppet-President Barack Obama, to have their way in health-care and other pet Obama "reforms."

Thus, if the U.S. economy is actually being destroyed out of the malice represented by puppet-like British instruments such as Barack Obama, say, "Scylla and Charybdis," as it is, presently; the present U.S. government and industry have the ability to destroy the United States through their malice; but, in general, they could not save it, if they would. The only world monetarist systems in which the United States and Europe functioned since March 1, 1968, are immediately doomed beyond hope; but, the reigning opinion has not a shred of intentional competence needed to save the world from a new dark age.

True, President Franklin Roosevelt saved civilization from a plunge into a dark age earlier. Something similar could have been done, as I had proposed in 2007. With what has happened since 2007, especially since the bail-outs of early 2009, only something much more drastic than a return to FDR, could rescue civilization today. Only the replacement of the world's monetary system by an Alexander Hamilton-style American constitutional form of credit-system could save any part, or all parts of global civilization today. This needed rescue needs much more than mere words on paper; it requires appropriate action. It requires the actions in policy-shaping for which I am the leading spokesman now.

Certain Very Hard Facts

The only actually available beginning of a general remedy for the presently accelerating, global, general physical-economic breakdown-crisis of both our re-

Library of Congress

It is long past time we returned to our Constitutional commitment to a credit system, specifically that which was embedded in our Constitution by our first Treasury Secretary, Alexander Hamilton, shown here in an 1861 engraving.

public and the world at large, lies in two mutually indispensable general measures of reform:

1.) Put the U.S. financial system through global reorganization in bankruptcy, writing off the mass of financial trash which has been accumulated under the leaderships of Alan Greenspan, Henry Paulson, Timothy Geithner, and the Obama crew generally, and transferring those assets consistent with the earlier Glass-Steagall standard from the accounts of a Federal Reserve-cued monetary system, into a resuscitation of our Federal constitutional absolute commitment to a credit-system in our patriotic Hamiltonian, constitutional tradition.

2.) That affirmation of our Federal Constitutional commitment to a credit-system, rather than a monetary system, will create the premises for bringing a selection of qualified leading nations of the planet into a pioneering action whose intent will be to bring the U.S.A.,

Russia, China, India, and certain other keystone-nations of a new global credit-system, into being, to replace the incurably rotten, existing world monetary system. Without writing off most of the pure financial trash encumbering the economies of the entire world today, no physical-economic recovery of the planet from the present, planetary process of collapse into a planetary "new dark age" would be possible.

But, we also need:

3.) The eradication of all international authority over the rule of this planet except that authority represented by a set of perfectly sovereign nation-state republics. The standard used for this purpose must therefore use the precedent of the post-World War II measures which President Franklin D. Roosevelt had intended, had he lived. The legacy of the Truman-Churchill, proneo-colonial betrayal of civilization on the occasion of President Franklin Roosevelt's death must be eradicated from the institutions of international cooperation among sovereign republics.

4.) The immediate adoption of the use of a new international credit-system, represented by perfectly sovereign nation-state republic, and the cancellation of measures of so-called "globalization," according to the principles of peace adopted according to the legacy of Cardinal Nicholas of Cusa, the principles of the 1648 Peace of Westphalia. The sovereign nation-state must be restored to its rightful place as the true agent of representation of its people and their tradition. and all marches in the direction of a new, London-steered "Tower of Babel" must be cancelled without exception. A system of protectionist measures in aid of this policy must be established by treaty agreements among perfect sovereigns.

5.) The sovereign nation-state republics of the planet must be engaged in an approximately fifty-year program of mobilization of national credit-systems for cooperation in urgently needed projects of basic economic infrastructure and development of industrial and agricultural productivity. The emphasis, from the start, must be large-scale, largely capital-intensive investments in basic-economic infrastructure throughout the planet, under a fixed-exchange-rate system of credit for the world as a whole. To achieve the intended goal, borrowing costs of between 1.5-2.0% simple interest shall be the standard for such investments in recapitalization of the greatly increased productive powers of labor per capita and per square kilometer throughout the world.

Retaking the Industrial Heartland For LaRouche's Four Laws

by Bill Roberts

Jan. 20—LaRouche PAC has now released a national statement, "2018 LaRouche PAC Election Platform: The Campaign to Win the Future," which defines the only sane political battleplan for American voters in the months ahead.

The key components of that 2018 LaRouche Platform are the following:

1) End the coup against the President and prosecute those responsible for the criminal frauds they have perpetrated.

2) Implement LaRouche's *Four New Laws* for Economic Recovery and bring the United States into full participation with China's Belt and Road Initiative for economic development.

In November 2016, the critical margin of victory for Donald Trump on election night was determined by an electoral shift in states in the industrial Midwest. As Lyndon LaRouche indicated at the time, this was part of a global shift in the world, a rejection of the failed policies of the trans-Atlantic financial system, including the destruction of the productive workforce of nations and useless, regime-change wars. In the period leading up to the election, Donald Trump campaigned heavily in traditionally blue mid-western states like Michigan and Wisconsin, while Hillary did not. To illustrate the gravity of the shift that occurred among segments of voters between 2008 and 2016, there were 206 counties nationally that voted for Barack Obama twice—in 2008 and 2012—and then voted for Donald Trump in 2016; 53% of those counties are located in the states of Illinois, Indiana, Iowa, Michigan, Minnesota, Missouri, Ohio, and Wisconsin.

Both parties are now eyeing competitive congressional districts, especially in these areas, hoping to swing the vote to gain more congressional seats in the

EDITORIAL

EIRNS/Susan Kokinda

Bill Roberts on Jan. 20, 2018, showing a map of U.S. counties that had previously voted for Obama, and then voted for Trump.

next election. However, neither party is providing solutions the country needs to address the dire economic needs of the forgotten men and women who helped elect Trump. A sane approach for the Democratic Party would be to recognize the treasonous nature of the Robert Mueller-led Russiagate coup, then to help end it, and work with Trump to pass the Glass-Steagall Act, and build great projects.

Instead, many of these Democrats continue to spout the now-exposed lies on Russiagate, while they simultaneously adopt a shifting anti-Trump narrative, ranging from Trump's supposed unfitness for office to the Dick Durbin-created lie that Trump uttered racist remarks. Thus, for many prospective Democratic Party candidates, they have absolutely nothing of substance to say, and their "campaigns" consist entirely of anti-Trump slanders and empty diatribes.

It is precisely these Obama-organized antics that have made Democratic representatives an endangered species among blue collar and rural districts across the Midwest.

On the Republican side, many among that Party's leadership continue to cling to Wall Street policies which will destroy the Trump Presidency and the nation. Wall Street-approved policies will never rebuild the areas devastated by the tropical storms of the past Summer or allocate the funding to stop the further crumbling of our infrastructure. Wall Street-controlled politicians will never move to shut down the illegal drug trade facilitated by those banks. They will only set up the next big, catastrophic debt bubble crash. Perhaps if the news media had reported the basic facts about President Trump's success in securing $254 billion in direct investment from Chinese companies into the United States, everyone would already be thinking about how China is able to do that while we spend hundreds of billions subsidizing Wall Street.

There is a *profound* vacuum of leadership waiting to be filled by those who exhibit a basic grasp of how the implementation of LaRouche's Four Economic Laws

LaRouche PAC organizing in Detroit.

EIRNS/Bill Roberts

will transform this nation's economy, opening up coordination among the credit systems of nations.

"Throw the bums out!" the disgusted citizen says of their Congress members. It seems many have already thrown themselves out. After at least 55 members of the U.S. House of Representatives have announced that they will not run for re-election, a record number of U.S. House elections will be open races, and may draw large and crowded fields of candidates. Some of them will be local and state representatives who have studied and supported the policy proposals of Lyndon LaRouche.

In traditionally Democratic districts, we may see Obama-backed candidates running against candidates actually interested in reviving skilled labor and farming. There will be races where the LaRouche PAC will be intervening to defeat incumbents who still openly associate themselves with the coup against the Presidency. We will insist that opposing candidates adopt the LaRouche platform, and that they campaign on it. The challenge for all of us is to create, in the constituencies of our districts, the notion that there is an option for using this LaRouche platform to create a standard of competence for the candidates running for federal office, whether they be Democrat, Republican, or Independent.

This author sat through a Republican candidates' debate which focused almost entirely on questions relating to immigration, and various other conservative hot-button issues. While candidates were asked how much they agreed with this or that policy of President Trump, none of those policies mentioned were the ones central to the crucial policy fight unfolding in the world. However, when I had the chance to speak to two of the candidates privately, both expressed a reverence for the wisdom of Lyndon LaRouche. One of them lamented that the Republican Party had made the critical mistake of abandoning cooperation with LaRouche, after Reagan left the Presidency and the Bush gang ran a political assassination against him.

In the last two weeks, LaRouche PAC teams have conducted a series of meetings with state legislators in state capitals across the nation. In those discussions, we have seen a seriousness and willingness to fight. They are determined to demand a national top-down solution. Many Democrats want to end the treasonous coup attempt against President Trump and work with him to rebuild the country. Republicans are willing to reach across the aisle to find ways to get large-scale federal funding for big projects and end the Wall Street bubble. State legislators who have traveled the world are amazed at how China's policies are transforming the face of the planet. They are intrigued, and have a sense of urgency that we must not miss the opportunity at hand. They know that the political parties are in shambles. The basis for a new national constituency—a coalition of producers—certainly exists.

Unfortunately, the election campaign process—aided and abetted by the mass media—is highly partisan in nature. Candidates are encouraged to play down to the lowest common denominator, the most base fears and desires of their imagined voter base. We have the power to change this! Not only should every opportunity be made to demand that these candidates campaign on the basis of LaRouche's Four Laws, but professional associations, labor unions, state legislatures, and advocacy groups should endorse the LaRouche PAC 2018 Election Platform and campaign for the policies contained therein. Thus, we will force the issue of the urgent need for a new Hamiltonian Credit System, as outlined by Lyndon LaRouche.